THE EPIC BOOK OF UNBELIEVABLE TRUE STORIES

Chili Mac Books

Table of Contents

BEFORE YOU BEGIN

Hey reader, as a thank you for grabbing a copy of the book, I wanted to offer you a bonus book.

I've collected some whacky WW2 stories you will not believe are true.

Even as I was digging these up, I didn't believe some of them either, but the research checks out.

I wrote this book for my WW2 buffs who just can't get enough about the Second World War.

To grab your free copy, scan the QR code below.

I can't wait to hear what you think!

INTRODUCTION

Would you believe that soldiers used to deliberately pee on their equipment? Would you believe that a World War II British commander played the bagpipes as his troops went into battle? Would you believe an SS agent is buried in Arlington National Cemetery? Would you believe ...

To all these questions as well as the others in this book – they all looked like tabloid headlines rather than factual stories to me when I first came across them - my initial reaction was an emphatic NO. NO WAY. NO. NO. NO. However, after careful research, I have discovered that each of the statements in the book are true – or at least have not been proven to be false.

Prepare to be educated; the articles are fact-based – I am not making this stuff up! Prepare to have fun; the stories are shared by myself, a folksy narrator with a great sense of humor and a gift for taking boring, complicated subjects and making them interesting and intelligible to the average person. Prepare to be amazed; these are gems that most schools forget to teach. In case you just can't accept what you are reading, references are provided so that you can do what I did – do further research into the matter until you are satisfied.

In this book you will find gallant examples of patriotism that will make you proud; you will find techniques that might save your life, such as how to unbury yourself if you are trapped by an avalanche of snow; and fascinating stories that you can share to amaze your friends and family at the next cocktail party or family gathering. This is a book you will want to return to again and again.

Would you believe ... we are ready to get into the book now?

CHAPTER 1

WOULD YOU BELIEVE...

AN ELECTRICIAN TURNED HIS CAR INTO A MOTORCYCLE WHILE STRANDED IN THE SAHARA DESERT?

"You don't stop riding when you get old,
you get old when you stop riding."
- Anonymous

ELECTRICIAN

Remember that exercise in elementary school in which the teacher said you were to pretend to be stuck in the desert and she asked you what you would bring? What did you reply? If you said a car with a broken axel, your teacher probably would have scoffed, but that is exactly what Emile Leray had, and he got back to civilization.

Emile Leray, a French electrician, found himself stranded in the middle of the Sahara Desert in Africa. He had tried to drive his Citroen 2CV - for those of you who have never seen the Citroen 2CV, it is very similar in shape and size to the Volkswagen Beetle - around a roadblock soldiers had put up to keep traffic from going further up the road where armies were shooting at each other.

To get around the roadblock, he had first turned around and pretended to be going home. Once he was out of the guards' shooting range, he spun the car off the road and into the desert sand. Emile knew the Citroen 2CV is known as "The Steel Camel" because it can go through the desert provided it is driven gently, and he was confident his vehicle would get him to his destination.

Did you catch the phrase "provided it was driven gently"? Emile was not driving his Citroen 2CV gently; he was flooring it so that he could get out of the security guards' view before they saw him. He drove fast and furious, and he succeeded in his goal of getting to where no one would find him; at first this was a relief. Then, though, it became a curse - he hit some bumps and broke an axel and a swingarm, and there was no one near him to offer assistance.

He took one look at the car and realized he could not fix it. He considered his options: He was too far from the security check to walk back in the desert heat. He was not on a road or even a path, and no one would just happen to come along. His friends wouldn't notice he was missing for a couple of days, and, when they did, they wouldn't know where to look. (This was 1993, and he didn't have a cell phone.) He appeared to have the option of walking through the sand and dying or staying where he was and dying - the result was the same.

Many people would have just given up and made their peace with death. Emile was not one of those people. After a good night's sleep and time to think, he set the body of the car aside to use as a hut and shelter. He then proceeded to tear, cut, and pry parts off the car with the goal of making a working motorcycle.

I have watched U.S. agent Angus MacGyver make use of technology and science on the fictional television show *MacGyver*, but even MacGyver's scriptwriters would have been hard-pressed to turn a car into a motorcycle. In fact, once Emile got back to civilization, the television show *MythBusters* tried to repeat the feat and could not think of how to turn the car into a motorcycle. The show's hosts became skeptical of Emile's story after their failure, but when they followed Emile's step-by-step directions, they were able to build a motorcycle just as he had done.

Emile estimated it would take three days to make the motorcycle and that he had ten days of water. When day twelve began, he had not finished, but he still had a little water. He finished the project that afternoon, fired it up - the engine started, the gears turned the wheels - and he was able to ride it back into civilization.

Now, I'd like to stop the story right there and say that the story had a happy ending. That, though, would not be telling you the whole story. The story does not end with the triumphant ride back into civilization on the bike he called the "Desert Camel". Instead, it has one last unexpected twist:

As Emile was cruising into town on the Desert Camel, he suddenly noticed that a patrol officer had pulled up behind him. Emile could see that the officer wanted him to pull over, so he did. The patrol officer sarcastically asked him if he knew he was operating an illegal vehicle. (Even the best of parades get rained on, don't they?) Welcome back to civilization, Emile!

CHAPTER 2

WOULD YOU BELIEVE . . .

SOME GARDEN FIGURES ARE REAL LIVING BEINGS?

"Life begins the day you start a garden."
– Chinese proverb

    I have had several interesting jobs in my time. For instance, I hawked programs at Arrowhead Stadium in Kansas City, Missouri, calling, "Program. Get your program here" to anyone who passed on their way to watch the Kansas City Chiefs play football. I also went door to door in towns across Illinois asking people to subscribe to a free newspaper. (It appears that the company had gotten in trouble for "littering" because they had thrown the newspaper to every driveway in these towns, and now they needed permission to throw it.)

+ + +

One job I have not had is a garden gnome. Yes, just like people who go door-to-door "selling" subscriptions to a free newspaper, these jobs do exist. Getting a job as a garden gnome is not as easy as it was a hundred years ago because there are not as many large estates, but the opportunity is still there. Most of us have probably seen those plastic garden gnomes with the goofy hats at the lawn-and-garden shop and/or a plastic table in a garden to suggest that a gnome exists, but, if someone has the money they don't have to settle for a silly statue or a suggestive table. Money can buy anything - including someone to live in a back-yard Paradise.

Job requirements and pay vary significantly from employer to employer. Some employers expect their live gnome to prep for weeks – letting their hair, fingers, and toenails grow out, refusing to bathe, and living in complete isolation. Room and board are almost always included; the garden gnome will be expected to live in a hut in the garden. In some gardens the garden gnome is allowed to speak to the guests and owners as they pass; in other gardens, the gnome is merely a living decoration and does not interact with anyone. Contracts can be very lucrative and range from a few days to several years; most garden gnomes get paid at the end of the agreed to period so if the garden gnome doesn't stay the whole time, the garden gnome doesn't earn a dime.

Being a garden gnome is the ultimate acting experience; the garden gnome must stay in character the entire time, even when the garden gnome thinks no one is looking. Besides actors who want to perfect their craft, the job of garden gnome is ideal for someone wanting to get away from it all; if being a hermit is on your bucket list, why not get paid for doing it?

Although some very rich folks live modestly and invest their money, the want-to-be rich are constantly flaunting their money. Having a living garden gnome is the pinnacle of flaunting money. Can you imagine going to a cocktail party and hearing one old biddy say, "In my garden, my gnome . . ." only to be one-upped by her friend, who counters, "That's nothing. My gnome . . ."

The closest I have come to being a professional gnome is being a mall Santa Claus. I was quite a trickster too. I often overheard kids talk as I walked through the mall in my street clothes and then, when I was in character as Santa and they came to visit me, I would remind them of what they had said. Santa magic was real for those kids for at least another year! I found it easy to stay in character for my four-hour shift in the chair and on the walk to and from the dressing room. Santa could do and say things that I could not; my girlfriend would have been very upset if sorority girls came to sit on my lap and got their picture taken with me in my street clothes, but when I was Santa, it didn't bother her. Although I enjoyed being Santa, I enjoy being me more. I personally would find it miserable to try to be somebody else for years and not have the freedom to be myself. I guess the gnome-culture just isn't for me.

CHAPTER 3

WOULD YOU BELIEVE . . .

POOR PEOPLE IN VICTORIAN LONDON WADED IN RIVERS OF FECES SEARCHING FOR COINS AND JEWELRY?

"Seventeen million gallons of that is sewage,
the rest is rainwater."
- Cory Crebbin

Do you enjoy playing Dungeons and Dragons or going on video quests with your friends? Do you enjoy the thrill of finding treasure; take pleasure in pulse-pounding life-and-death struggles; and crave working in teams? If you answered yes to these questions, you would have made a good sewer hunter in Victorian London.

Sewer hunters - generically known as part of the toshers, groups that scavenged at the waterfront, sewers, or the dumps - wandered the underground caverns of London from the days of King Henry VIII until 1840 when wandering the tunnels was made illegal. (The authorities say that sewer hunters ceased existing in 1840 because sewer hunting was made illegal, but just between you and me, I don't believe it. Just because something is illegal doesn't mean that it still wasn't done; if you don't believe this is possible, consider the liquor and marijuana laws of today and how well those prohibitions are obeyed by today's youth.)

+ + +

A sewer hunter could enter the sewer on one's own, but typically sewer hunters traveled in groups of three or four. The London sewers were underground and, although sometimes a light peeped through a drain from above, many parts of the sewers were pitch-black and at least 40-feet underground. Although sewer hunters didn't know exactly what they would encounter when exploring a sewer, they knew danger lurked around each corner in the sewer tunnels – the danger might be a group of rats waiting to attack, a sinkhole in which one could fall, or a mugger. To defend themselves, sewer hunters would carry a hoe. The hoe could be used as a club against a rat or as an extension of one's arm to grab onto something if one started to sink. Sewer hunters also had to be on guard for rising tides, for many of the thousand-plus miles of piping filled completely with water at high tide.

Sewer hunters had lanterns that clipped to their body, freeing one hand to carry the hoe and the other hand to feel the ground for possible treasure. One of the advantages of traveling in groups was better lighting. A second advantage to groups was that the guide leading the group had usually been in the tunnel system many times and knew both the shortest routes and the most lucrative routes.

In addition to the hoe and the lantern, a prospective sewer hunter needed to invest in a backpack, a place to put any treasure that was found. Although most of what sewer hunters came across was dead animals, human waste, industrial byproducts, and other toshers who had either drowned or become rat food, the sewer hunters also came across coins, dropped rings, and dropped necklaces. It wasn't the Sewer Fairy that put the coins and jewelry in the sewer; people would accidently drop coins and jewelry into the street, rainwater would wash the coins and jewelry into the drain system, and then the current would sweep the coins and jewelry downstream. A good tosher knew where

in the sewer these products would likely settle and would check those places regularly just as you and I might check a mouse trap waiting for the mouse to appear. Typical sewer hunters made more income in a given day than many middle-class people, and sewer hunters considered themselves a notch above the other scavengers. If a sewer hunter could resist the temptation to drink and managed to stay alive in the sewers, the sewer hunter could eventually rise in society.

I see people today with metal detectors on the beach hoping to find lost coins; they have unusual, tosher-like jobs. Likewise, I see people raiding the dumpsters for items that have been designated trash by someone else; the raiders will then take these items to the flea market or an auction house and try to liquidate them. Also, our society still has people who go to the local dump to marvel at how other people have thrown away quality items. I myself pick up cans in the name of recycling - all right, who am I kidding - I pick them up as a way to raise beer money, but it still helps the environment. While it may be tempting to look down on sewer hunters, I don't. Most of my friends and I are similar to the sewer hunters - we all started with a humbling job such as waiting tables or mowing yards as we strived to save to go to college and make it in the professional world. The sewer hunters literally had a lousy job - and I thought it was bad coming home smelling like French fries when I worked fast food - but it was an honest living, and their perseverance and desire to move upward is worthy of respect.

CHAPTER 4

WOULD YOU BELIEVE...

FROZEN POOP CAN BE USED AS A CHISEL?

"A sculptor wields the chisel,
and the stricken marble grows to beauty."
- William Cullen Bryant

Some people are full of poop, making up tall-tales and telling lies. Other people are literally full of poop, passing gas and leaving behind a piece of themselves wherever they go. Once in a while, these two groups overlap, producing someone who tells poop about poop. This happened twice around 1953.

In the first case, an elderly Inuit man was asked to give up his igloo and move to the village with his family. When the man refused, his family took all his tools, figuring he would have no choice but to come. The man, though, was a survivor. He defecated outside the igloo and molded the poop into a knife. (When life gives you lemons, you make lemonade; when life gives you poop, you make a knife.) To make the knife sharp, he added spit. Once the knife was frozen, he used the rock-hard, razor-sharp weapon to kill a dog. He then used the dead

dog's skin to make a harness and the ribcage to make a sled. He captured another dog, harnessed it to the sled, and set out into the darkness. His grandson who talked to the reporter for this story couldn't vouch for the details, but he did know his grandpa was never seen by family or friends again, and he believed the story to be true.

A second case of a poop knife happened around the same time. Peter Freuchen, a Danish explorer of the Artic, was exploring Greenland when his whole world caved in on him - literally. An avalanche fell down the mountainside and buried him alive in a cocoon of ice. Without anything to grip to pull himself out of the snow, Peter's life appeared to be over. Peter had an idea, though; he would create a knife from poop to use as a chisel. Peter took a dump and molded the resulting excrement with the same care as a blacksmith. He was inside the icy tomb 30 hours making his knife and chiseling, and it took him another three hours to crawl back to his encampment. Months later, back in Europe, Peter shared the story of his escape, and he became a celebrity.

Many people accepted these stories as facts - no questions asked, but other people were much more skeptical. Researchers at Kent University decided to test if human feces could be frozen and, if so, if it would cut. (Scientists in the real world get to do the neatest things, don't they? When I was in school, the most we got to do was dissect a frog and watch a seed bloom in a Dixie cup.)

To make sure they were being fair to the outdoorsmen, one of the researchers ate the explorer's diet for weeks, making sure to have lots of meats and proteins. Meanwhile, to determine if the average person could make a poop knife, the other researcher ate their typical American diet. After a month, they collected plastic bags of their poop, molded knives from the

poop, and froze the knives using dry ice. The researchers didn't want to kill a dog, so they found a pig hide and attacked it. Although the frozen knives were rock solid, they did not cut deep into the hide; they just left poop skid marks where the poop melted from the heat of the motion. The first story was a hoax!

The second story is also likely a hoax, but the researchers admit that using a poop knife as a knife to scrape and using it as a chisel are slightly different, so there is a slim chance Peter was telling the truth. Poop knives certainly don't make the cut - pun intended, and the odds of a poop knife serving as a wedge are very slim. Hopefully you are never in an avalanche in the Arctic, but life has a way of taking some strange twists and turns, so, if you find yourself under an avalanche always remember that there is a chance you may be able to become a 3-D printer and poop out the solution to your problem.

CHAPTER 5

WOULD YOU BELIEVE...

A STEWARDESS FELL OVER 33,000 FEET WITH NO PARACHUTE - AND SURVIVED?

"Minds are like parachutes -
they only function when open."
– Thomas Dewar

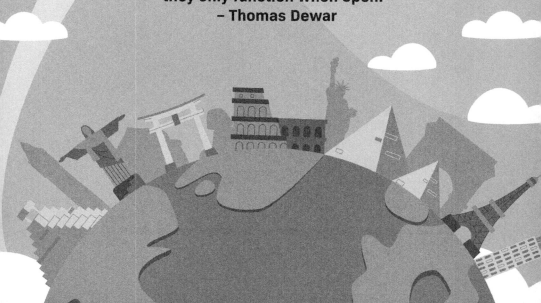

Can you believe that a 22-year-old stewardess named Vesna fell 33,316.8 feet - that is 6.31 miles - without a parachute - and lived? I would say that she lived to talk about it, but I would be lying, for she honestly doesn't remember it happening and therefore can't talk about it.

She wasn't even supposed to be on the Jat Airways flight; some other girl named Vesna was. When the supervisors realized the two girls shared the same name and that the other Vesna was not arriving on time - or at all - they asked if she, Vesna Vulovic, would be willing to go to Denmark, take the afternoon and evening to shop and sightsee, and then be on another flight the next morning. Vesna, a native of Serbia, preferred going to England - she

+ + +

had gotten into flying earlier that year to go to England because she idolized the Beatles and she wanted to learn about England; however, she had never been to Denmark, so she accepted the opportunity.

That afternoon and evening, Vesna and her friends shopped; Vesna had wanted to sight-see, but the rest were adamant about shopping. The next day at 2:30 p.m., they boarded a Jat Airways DC-9 which had just touched down from Stockholm at the Copenhagen Airport. At 3:15 p.m., the plane, named Flight 367, left the Copenhagen Airport. At 4:01 p.m., an explosion went off in the baggage compartment, causing the aircraft to break apart over Czechoslovakia. (Upon reflecting, Vesna and others did see a nervous man exit the plane at Copenhagen and not get back on; the authorities suspect he was a Croatian terrorist, but no arrests have ever been made.

Vesna, the 28 passengers and the other crew members fell to the ground like pieces of candy from a broken tube. Only Vesna survived the 6.25 mile fall, and that was due to five factors coming together: (1) she had low blood pressure, so she had passed out, allowing her heart not to be stressed; (2) her foot got caught on a dessert cart in the fuselage and so she did not spill out of the plane; (3) the fuselage landed on a snowy carpet, cushioning the impact; (4) someone found her; (5) that someone was Bruno Honke, a former medic, who was able to keep her alive until ambulances arrived.

To say that she had some injuries is an understatement. She fractured her skull, hemorrhaged, and spent several days in a coma. She broke three vertebrae, both legs, and several ribs, as well as fractured her pelvis. All of this meant she was temporarily paralyzed from the waist down. She had total amnesia; the last thing she remembered before the crash was greeting passengers as they boarded; her next memory was seeing her parents in her hospital room a month later.

Two weeks into her hospital stay, she was told about the crash. She was so horrified that she had to be tranquilized. However, she loved flying so much that, once she was well enough to go back to work - September 1972, she asked to resume her stewardess duties. Jat Airlines, though, believed she would be perceived as a celebrity and that passengers would not give her time to perform those duties, so they gave her a desk job.

In 1985, she was officially recognized by the *Guinness Book of World Records* as the highest jumper without a parachute; that award was presented by the former Beatle, Paul McCartney, at a London musical gala. Things had truly come full-circle for her, a true revolution.

CHAPTER 6

WOULD YOU BELIEVE . . .

A MAN STOLE A TANK
AND LED POLICE ON A CHASE THROUGH SAN DIEGO?

"The police are not here to create disorder,
they're here to preserve disorder."
- Richard J. Daley

How do you deal with your anger and frustration? Do you hit a punching bag? Do you meditate? Do you scream at the top of your lungs? All of these are common coping mechanisms. One thing you don't likely do, though, is take a tank on a joy ride.

Shawn Nelson was an angry, amphetamine-addicted, unemployed plumber. In his mind, he had good reason to be angry - at God, at the government, at his wife, at the hospital, and at people in general. He had lost his parents within the span of five years and was seething about the care they had received. He himself had been hospitalized following a motorcycle wreck; he sued the hospital for negligence, but he lost his case; to make things worse, the hospital had counter-sued wanting him to pay their legal fees and the bill he did not believe he owed. His wife was a legal secretary and they had enjoyed six good years of

marriage, but she had left him when the pills became the focus of his life. When someone had stolen his plumbing tools, he had lost his way to make an income. With the electricity to his house turned off and the foreclosure date on his house set, Shawn drove his Chevy van to the National Guard Armory in San Diego on May 17, 1995.

No one knows for sure why he went there. Did he go there to seek help, or did he go there to steal a tank? The bottom line is, when his eyes lit upon the Patton tanks sitting there, Shawn knew he had to have one. Shawn was an honorably discharged veteran, and he knew how to drive a tank. The tanks at the armory did not require keys; they just needed the push of a button. The first two tanks did not start, but the third did. As he started the engine, a soldier saw him and called for him to stop. Shawn ignored the soldier and drove the tank onto the street.

Shaw enjoyed releasing tension that day. He drove the tank over a fire hydrant and watched the water shoot out. He ran over pedestrians' cars and could hear the metal crush beneath him. He was soon being followed by squad cars, but the police did not have the means to disable a tank, so all they could do was follow and watch. Shawn was driving at top speed - about 30 miles per hour; he led the police onto the south-bound lanes of State Route 163.

Shawn had the road to himself; the south-bound lane had been cleared to keep citizens as safe as possible. When Shawn came across a bridge, he struck the bridge's pillar again and again. The cement did not give, however, and Shawn went under the bridge and down the road. Shawn next tried to cross the concrete median that divided the north-bound traffic from the south-bound, but the 57-ton tank got stuck trying to climb over the concrete barrier.

Did Shawn have a destination in mind or was he simply joyriding, not even thinking about the future? Those who say he had a destination claim he was likely on his way to the hospital. Shawn had a lot of weapons - a 105-millimeter cannon, a 12.7-millimeter anti-aircraft gun, and a 7.62-millimeter machine gun, but did not have any ammunition; they kept the ammunition in a separate building in the armory, and Shawn had not had time to load any. Loaded weapons or not, as he had demonstrated with the crushed cars he left behind the tank itself could do considerable damage.

Shawn jumped up and down inside the tank, trying to wiggle the tank off the median barrier. With the tank stopped, the police were able to climb onto the tank. A former Marine sergeant used bolt cutters to open the hatch and demanded Shawn surrender. When Shawn kept trying to free the tank, his partner brought the tank-thief's half-hour joy-ride - and life - to an end.

Why did he do it? Perhaps Shawn committed suicide-by-cop while making a public statement about hospital care. Perhaps it was drug-induced insanity. Regardless of why he did it, the metaphor of a man in a tank attacking the civilization he once protected because he is so disillusioned with it, is an image that is not easily forgotten. Everybody has rage - you too, admit it - and we too must find a way to work through that rage.

CHAPTER 7

WOULD YOU BELIEVE . . .

LOVELY LADIES USED THEMSELVES AS LEECH BAIT?

"A leech that will not quit the skin
until sated with blood"
- Horace

Call me crazy, but I think the Kansas City Chiefs professional football team's fate rests in my hands even though I am hundreds of miles from the stadium. When I sit in front of the television watching the game, the team tends to win. When I go to the kitchen to make a sandwich, they tend to lose. If I am not in the living room doing my part, they are not going to win. That sounds crazy, doesn't it, and yet I can show you time after time after time where this has happened. Can we take a chance that it is just coincidence and superstition? I tell my wife that I need to be watching just in case it is true - the whole town is depending on me. If she insists that I mow the yard or do other household chores on game day, the team is going to crumble, and it will be my fault - I don't know if I can live with the guilt.

My experience of influencing the team from my house is similar to what happened in the medical profession in the early and mid-1800s, when doctors used leeches to suck out "bad" blood from patients. If you had a boil, both patients and doctors thought that letting a leech suck out the bad blood was important. If you had an illness, both patients and doctors believed a leech could help get your blood back in balance. The leeches may not have actually worked – in fact, they often lead to death – but both doctors and patients had seen patients recover after having their blood sucked by a leech, so they believed the leeches made a difference.

Medical fads come and go. Remember how popular the Atkins Diet was a few years ago? I personally liked the Drive-Thru Diet sponsored by Taco Bell. These fads are presented with great hype, but, eventually, people realize they don't work, or a new diet comes along with new hype that attracts everyone. The medical field is evolving rapidly, and even the best medical solution of today may be sub-par after additional breakthroughs are discovered.

In the 1800s, leeches were used both externally and internally. (I've heard of people having a bug up their butt, but these patients had actual leeches.) The doctor would place the leech on - or in, as the case might be - the designated area, make sure the leech is attached, and then let the leech enjoy an all-you-can-eat meal. The leech would take 20 minutes to a few hours to gorge itself with the patient's blood. The leech was then scraped off the body with the doctor's fingernail or a sharp instrument. If anything, the leeches killed people, but, because people often got better - no thanks to the leeches - the leeches were credited with the success and became further entrenched in medical use. By the 1870s doctors realized leeches did not work in most cases, but patients had "seen them work," and upon the patients' insistence, the practice of using leeches continued into the early 1900s.

Did you realize that someone had to provide these leeches; the doctor didn't grow them in his little black bag. Being a leech gatherer could be a full-time profession. People who could gather 500 or more leeches in a given day could make a middle-class income. Leech gathering, though, was hard work, and the middle-class, of course, avoided it. (Leeches suck!) middle-class income.

To gather leeches, one had to go to leech-infested waters. If one wanted to be proactive, one could beat the weeds of the swamp to stir them up and then catch the leeches, but leech gatherers found it was much easier to let the leeches come to them. By putting their legs in the water, the leech gatherers would attract the leeches. Leeches would attach themselves to the legs and suck their blood; the leech collector usually needed to wait until the leech was full to attempt to remove it, otherwise one would open up a huge wound because the leech was not going to let go willingly. If the leech collector had an old horse, the leech collector could have the horse walk into the water and use it as leech bait instead of one's own body- but most leech gatherers didn't have an old horse. (Many leech collectors were young women, and, in an age when even a woman's ankle was forbidden for a man to see, the site of girls hanging their limbs in the water with leeches feasting on them was both provocative and abhorrent.)

Once the leech was removed from one's body, it was placed in a canvas bag the leech collector carried. The wound from the leech would often continue to bleed, and this served to readily attract more leeches. Although people at the time may have thought that having leeches suck on one's body was a good thing, the leech collector ran the risk of losing too much blood and/or getting an infection. (Leeches are ugly, but if you have ever gone leech gathering, you know that they kind of grow on you. My friend cleaned out a pond, and he came home with a pet leech; it was very attached to him. I had to admit, the leech was very clingy.)

The leech catcher is a profession that has come and gone - today's leeches for medical purposes are farm-raised. That's right; I said that doctors are still using leeches today. Leeches are no longer seen as a remedy for everything, but they are still being used. The Kansas City Chiefs, meanwhile, continue to play football and - to my wife's frustration - I continue to stay in my chair watching them. Are we as a society still a superstitious lot - or are there some underlying cause-and-effect principles at work that we have yet to figure out?

CHAPTER 8

WOULD YOU BELIEVE . . .

BRUCE LEE'S SON FOLLOWED HIS DAD'S FOOTSTEPS OF BLENDING MARTIAL ARTS WITH HOLLYWOOD – AND DYING RIGHT BEFORE HIS BREAKOUT FILM?

"When you follow your dreams, you encourage
other people to follow theirs."
- Nafessa Williams

Like father; like son.

Kung Fu legend Bruce Lee died at the age of 33 right before the release of his breakthrough film. What would be the odds of his son doing the exact same things - being a karate expert, being a professional actor, dying before turning 33, and dying right before his breakout film hit the screens? Almost nil - that's why some people believe in the family curse.

Brandon Lee was eight years old when his dad, Bruce Lee, died. His dad had seemed in perfect health and had just made *Enter the Dragon*. One day while negotiating the details of his next film, Bruce developed a headache, took a painkiller, and finished his work schedule. He went home and laid down; his family could not rouse him at supper. He was then rushed to the hospital, where it was determined he had died from fluid on the brain, likely an allergic reaction to the painkiller. The cause of his death was ruled "misadventure."

Brandon was Bruce Lee's only son. (Jokesters have asked me "Who is Bruce Lee's vegetarian son" and, when I reply I do not know, they reply, "Brock Lee," but I can assure you that Brandon is his only son. Similarly, all those other Lees that you have heard of - Vague Lee, Quick Lee, Simp Lee, Sudden Lee, and Immediate Lee - are not Brandon's siblings either.) Brandon closely followed in his dad's footsteps, becoming a superb martial artist and then an actor. In fact, his career was not only on the same path as his dad's career had traveled; he was accomplishing the same things quicker. Whereas Bruce had been 33 when he made his breakout film, at 28, Brandon Lee was almost ready to release his breakout film - *The Crow*.

Just as his father had done on the day he died, Brandon went to work on his death day, having no idea that the day would be his last. Brandon was filming scenes instead of negotiating details of upcoming scenes. *The Crow*, a story about a man coming back to life from the undead to avenge his murder and that of his girlfriend, was just about to finish filming. In one of his last scenes in *The Crow*, Brandon's character was supposed to walk into an apartment where four thugs were attacking a woman; one of the thugs was to shoot him at close range. Unknown to anybody, the bullet in the so-called prop gun still had powder in the so-called blank cartridge, and when his coworker Michael Masse shot him at point-blank range just as the script required, the bullet pierced his side. After being shot, Brandon fell differently than the script directed, but nobody panicked: the director thought it was improv acting - or just clowning around. However, when time passed and Brandon didn't move, people became concerned. When his coworkers saw real blood, they rushed to call an ambulance; Brandon was taken to a nearby hospital where hours of operations were performed on him - but to no avail.

The Crow was finished using stunt doubles and special effects, and the movie went on to receive critical acclaim. With Brandon's death, the acting Bruce Lee family dynasty came to an end - and with it, apparently, the curse. Brandon had no children (although the gun that killed him was loaded, he himself apparently shot blanks), and his four-year younger sister Shannon, while she has followed in the tradition of blending martial arts with Hollywood, has yet to produce a breakthrough film.

I don't know if you believe in family curses or not. I do know that some family traditions just aren't worth carrying on. I also know that some achievements do seem to be cursed in our society. For instance, if you want to be guaranteed of dying in the next few months, all you have to do is win the "Oldest Person Alive" award; if you don't believe me, watch the news and it is almost certain the next recipient will die within literally a few months, sometimes days, of getting the award. Coincidence? Maybe, but it happens every time.

CHAPTER 9

WOULD YOU BELIEVE . . .

HARRY HOUDINI DIED FROM TWO PUNCHES TO THE GUT?

"I'm tired of fighting, Dash.
I guess this thing is going to get me."
- Harry Houdini

Harry Houdini considered himself to be an entertainer; the world considered Harry Houdini to be an illusionist. Harry was a real-life Dick Tracy who seemed indestructible, and, although some of his tricks were indeed tricks, much of what he did was skill. He had the skill to get out of a strait jacket and the skill to escape from a locked box that had been tossed in the ocean. He had escaped a dead whale's carcass, as well as from death row in a seemingly impregnable cell. People had seen him swallow 100 pins and needles and then pull them back from his mouth. People even swore they saw him grab a speeding bullet. He was tough, he was tricky, and - on October 31, 1926 - he was dead.

Harry was the most popular star of his generation. Not only was he a great entertainer, but he was also a prime example of the American dream. He had immigrated from Hungary in the early 1900s and had become a national celebrity. He was in high demand, and he was privy to conversations with very high-ranking people. He was living the dream - he was the dream. Now he was dead.

Dead. What killed him? Was it a trick that went wrong? No. Society has been told that he died from internal organ damage - and there is no doubt that he did have internal organ damage, but many people question if that is the real reason. Two weeks before he died, Harry broke his ankle when a piece of equipment hit it during an underwater escape. (Remember this seemingly unimportant detail; it will become important in the end.) One week before he died, Harry was speaking to a school class about his performances. Harry didn't give away his tricks - he even refused to patent them for fear someone would read about how they were done; however, Harry loved being in front of an audience and teasing it. He made a comment in a class that one of his so-called secrets was that he had tough stomach muscles; not convinced of what Harry was saying, one of his skeptic's sucker-punched him twice in the abdomen when he was not expecting it before Harry left the school. Harry may not have left the school with any hard feelings, but he certainly left with a major pain in his stomach; the punches apparently ruptured his appendix. Harry performed his show that evening and then went to the hospital later that night. A week later, Harry was declared dead.

Did the paragraph about being from Hungary, living in the 1910s, and having access to conversations with high-ranking people raise any red flags for you? If you know your world history, it likely did. If you don't know your history, don't be too ashamed. (In the rural school I attended, history was taught as an afterthought - the basketball coach had to have classes to justify being on faculty, so he was given history classes. Needless to say, we learned a lot more about basketball than history.) Recall that World War I began when the archduke of Austria-Hungary was assassinated; Austria-Hungary then attacked Serbia for sponsoring the attack; Russia then attacked Austria-Hungary because it attacked Serbia; and then Germany attacked Russia because Russia had attacked Austria-Hungary. Now do you grasp why many people think it was more than two punches in the gut that killed Harry? Harry Houdini was from Hungary, and he likely had sympathy for the Central powers during World War I. Now recall that Harry Houdini had access to people few other people had access to. Harry Houdini likely heard many high-level conversations at the parties he attended, and – give people a drink or two and they usually loosen up - he likely heard things that were not supposed to be public knowledge. Harry Houdini had access to very valuable secrets, and very well may have been a spy.

Did Harry Houdini die from a freak accident resulting from a stomach punch, or was he poisoned? Harry had escaped prison, but Harry was unable to escape the hospital. Remember that broken ankle we talked about earlier - it prevented his escape.

It has been almost 100 years since his death, and no definitive answer about the cause of his death has been given. Officially, he died from stomach punches, but it has remained so controversial that even the History Channel has dedicated shows to both make and disprove the case. Harry had escaped death literally a thousand times, but death ultimately claimed him. Death though, may not have been able to do it on his own - Death may have needed help to get the job done.

CHAPTER 10

WOULD YOU BELIEVE . . .

BLUEPRINTS FOR A SECOND PARIS - AN EXACT TWIN WITH ITS OWN EIFFEL TOWER - HAVE BEEN CREATED AND A COUNTRY HAS BEEN DETERMINED IN WHICH TO BUILD IT?

"Paris is always a good idea."
- Audrey Hepburn in "Sabrina"

Have you ever seen a diamond shimmer? Have you ever flown above a city at night? To me, the two look very similar - the city looks like a diamond shimmering. Inside the city there may be crimes in process, a flash flood taking place, and general mayhem occurring in the streets, but from thousands of feet in the air, the city looks so peaceful.

As World War I progressed through to 1918, French statisticians realized that this shimmering night view was the view that German pilots would have when they flew over Paris to drop their bombs and create chaos. The Germans had been bombing Paris for months during the day, but now that the French had installed anti-aircraft guns the Allies knew that the Germans would no longer fly missions in daylight. The Allies didn't expect the German bombings to stop completely, but they did predict the missions would be only at night under the cover of darkness when the anti-aircraft guns would not be nearly as effective.

The German bombing might not be as effective either, but it was still a bombing, and those bombs meant a loss of French lives and also severe damage to the 2000-year-old city's structures. Although the anti-aircraft guns meant a relief from much bombing, they were not enough to deter all further German attacks. The Allies racked their brains for ways to prevent the bombings entirely but could think of nothing. Finally, convinced there was no way to stop the bombings, they began to ponder how to minimize the damage.

Various ideas were suggested, but the one that the group decided to pursue was the most elaborate idea of all - to build a twin Paris next to the real Paris. Because the Germans would not be able to see the intricate details of the city any longer, there was a 50% chance that the pilot would mistake the fake Paris for the real Paris. During World War I, precision maps and sophisticated radar did not exist as they do today; the Germans had to rely on landmarks. (I have heard of stunt doubles who look identical to the star actor and who do the tough action scenes, but who would have thought that a city could have a stunt double?)

The fake Paris, named Paris Mark Deux, would not need people; people were too small to see from a German bomber. The city, though, would need rows of lights, replicas of large buildings, railroad tracks, rivers, roads, and other landmarks the Germans used for references. The Allies' plans show that the fake Paris was to be built on the Seine River and would have three sections - a suburbia area, the area of major landmarks such as the Eiffel Tower, and an area of fictional factories. The result would not be completely to scale, but it would look so closely like the real Paris that German pilots would question themselves as to which was the real Paris.

Did you notice that this project was approved in early 1918? If you remember your history, you'll recall that the war ended in November 1918 with an armistice; therefore, although the Allies' plans for the life-sized model of Paris were drawn and details were planned, the city was never developed. The technology, though, was used in World War II, such as building a fake factory by the real factory, so the Germans' odds of striking the real target were decreased.

Today, there is officially only one Paris, but, in reality, there are two - the Paris that lives in people's imagination and the Paris that exists in reality. The Paris of the imagination is the diamond that glitters at night; this is the Paris that attracts youth, intellectuals, and travelers. The real Paris is like any other large metropolitan area; it just has signs written in French instead of one's native language. People come to see the first, but usually find the second; after a couple of drinks, the two blend into one double vision, and that becomes the Paris one remembers.

CHAPTER 11

WOULD YOU BELIEVE . . .

ONE MAN ESCAPED FROM PRISON FOUR TIMES – HIS TOOLS WERE A WIRE, A SOUP BOWL, AND MISO SOUP?

"It is better that ten guilty escape than one innocent suffer."
- William Blackstone

Do you ever find yourself sometimes rooting for the bad guy as you watch television? For instance, do you cheer for Robin Hood and Jesse James? I admit that I do. Both of these men stole from the rich and then gave the money to the people whom they felt rightly deserved it; somehow, stealing from the evil rich made their stealing seem like much less of a crime. The truth is, sometimes the bad guys are anti-heroes; they are men who disobey laws, and yet we still root for them.

A modern anti-hero is Yoshie Shiratori. Yoshie would be the first to tell you that he was a bad man - he was a gambler and he killed people. As with most criminals, it was just a matter of time before he ended up in jail - and, sure enough, he got caught. While there is no doubt that Yoshie was a bad man, a case can be made that the people who guarded the Japanese prisons were even more wicked than he was. Like many other prisoners, Yoshie looked for ways to escape prison, not because he didn't want to serve his time,but because he wanted to escape the abuse dealt by the guards. One day, Yoshie found a wire in a bathroom cleaning kit; he used it to pick the lock on his handcuffs, then, when the guards weren't looking, he slipped out of prison.

The police found him three days later and put him back in the prison system. He was placed in a different facility, but the guards were equally as cruel, so Yoshie had no desire to stay in this prison either. As he sat in his cell, he noticed an air vent on the wall near the ceiling. By literally climbing the walls - prison will make you do that - he was able to reach the air vent; he determined that the cover of the vent was too tight for him to remove it. By making the walls vibrate by kicking them over many weeks, though, he was able to vibrate the cover of the vent loose enough to unhinge it. He then escaped through the air vent.

Yoshie's freedom did not last long; he was brilliant at finding ways to escape but not so great at keeping out of jail. He had only one friend and he went to stay with him - that friend just happened to be the only nice guard at his previous prison. The guard felt obligated to send Yoshie back to the prison system.

This time, Yoshie was sent to an "inescapable" prison. Yoshie didn't believe all the "inescapable" hype. He took it as a challenge to escape, and he quickly lit upon a plan. If you were to ask the guards about him, they would have said he was a model prisoner but that he had a strange quirk - he always made a big deal about the miso soup he was served, spitting it on his cell door in disgust. What the guards didn't realize is that the salt from the soup was corroding the gate, making its metal bendable. In time, the cell gate was so corroded that Yoshie was able to remove a piece and, having dislocated his shoulder, squeezed himself through the hole.

His freedom did not last long, though, and he was shortly back in jail. This time he had six armed guards assigned to him and he was under observation 24 hours per day seven days per week every week of the year. The walls were slick, and the ceiling was designed so that no one could reach it. The guards were so confident that they let Yoshie roam in the cell without handcuffs, daring him to try to escape. The judge gave him a motive to escape too - he would die in prison otherwise. Yoshie took them up on the challenge, but he had to admit that the ceiling was impregnable. Instead, he used a bowl as a shovel and gradually dug a tunnel. Although guards had been assigned to watch him, he made sure that watching him was as exciting as watching paint dry when the guards were looking, so the guards often distracted themselves with other activities, giving him plenty of opportunity to dig.

This time Yoshie got away - and he probably could have stayed away. However, his conscience got the better of him. He knew that he owed a debt to society, and he wanted to pay it. When a policeman showed him kindness by letting him bum a cigarette, he introduced himself - he was quite a celebrity in both the general public and law enforcement - and offered to turn himself in. The policeman accepted his offer. At the resulting trial, the judge understood why he had escaped so many times and, because he had come back willingly, his prison sentence was turned into 20 years. Yoshi didn't even have to do the twenty years, however; he was a model prisoner, and he was let out shortly for good behavior.

Yoshie was released from prison when he was 51. He worked odd jobs and reunited with his daughter. He had twenty good years as a free man. His exploits are still celebrated in Japan today. The book *Hagok* recounts his adventures. A memorial to him is kept in the Abashiri Prison Museum, one of the prisons he escaped from.

Is it right to root for murderers? I don't think so. However, is it right that murderers are treated inhumanely or that, once they have paid for their crime, they keep the label of criminal? I personally don't think that's right either. Although I know that Yoshie was a murderer fully deserving of prison, I found myself rooting for Yoshie to escape, and I bet you did too! Bad guys can be heroes!

CHAPTER 12

WOULD YOU BELIEVE . . .

A 15-FOOT-HIGH WAVE OF BEER FLOODED LONDON STREETS IN 1814?

"Floods are acts of God,
but flood losses are largely acts of man."
- Gilbert F. White

And on the sixth day God spaketh to Noah and said, "Noah, I am going to flood the world."

Noah replied, "Good God, after the ark-incident, you promised not to send another flood."

"All right then, not the world, just one corner of it; just enough so that people get the idea that I'm not happy with them. I'll even choose an area known for prostitutes and criminals."

Noah replied, "But Lord, you said you would not ever flood the world with water out of anger. You even sent your rainbow as a sign."

God relented, and replieth, "All right, I won't use water. I'll use beer."

Thus, in 1814, in the slums of London, 15-foot waves of alcohol filled the streets. Eight people drowned in St. Giles, London, England, and the basements of nearby shops filled with beer.

Take or leave the supernatural elements, the bottom line is that there really was a flood in St. Giles in 1814, and the flood was of beer, not water. The beer, a brown porter ale similar to stout brew, came from The Horseshoe Brewery. In 1810, The Horseshoe Brewery had installed a 22-foot-tall wooden fermentation tank; the tank contained 3,500 barrels of beer. The wooden staves of the tank were held together with iron rings. Now, 3,500 barrels-worth of beer pressing against the wood and iron is a lot of pressure. Also, over time, iron rusts and becomes softer. With all of that pressure and with the metal weakening, it was just a matter of time before a ring broke - but no one realized that.

On October 17, 1814, four years after the tank had been installed, one of the rings broke. That put pressure on the other rings, which in turn made them rupture, sending 320,000 gallons of beer through the streets. The fifteen-foot wave of beer rolled down George and New streets, picking up debris as it went. Three brewery workers were rescued from the waist-high flood; another got swept along but got pulled out of the rubble. Some people were not so lucky. The beer flooded an Irish wake, killing four mourners. A barmaid was trapped inside a tavern and got killed by debris slamming into her body. Two people were having tea when the beer flooded their basement, causing the house to collapse on them. In all, eight people died that day. Another person died from the incident but not from the flood - he was one of many that began to put the beer in cups and jars for future use or simply began to lap the beer like dogs - he died of alcohol poisoning.

If God, who is known for working in mysterious ways and for changing water into wine, is behind this, he certainly has a sense of humor. I hope he enjoys the above article and doesn't find it blasphemous. I want him to look at it and say, "Well done, good and faithful servant." Whether he is truly responsible or not, he is getting the credit by secular authorities - they all say The Great Beer Flood was an act of God!

CHAPTER 13

WOULD YOU BELIEVE . . .

BUBBLE WRAP WAS CREATED TO BE WALLPAPER, NOT FOR MAILING PACKAGES?

"Therapy is extremely expensive.
Popping bubble wrap is radically cheap."
- Jimmy Buffett

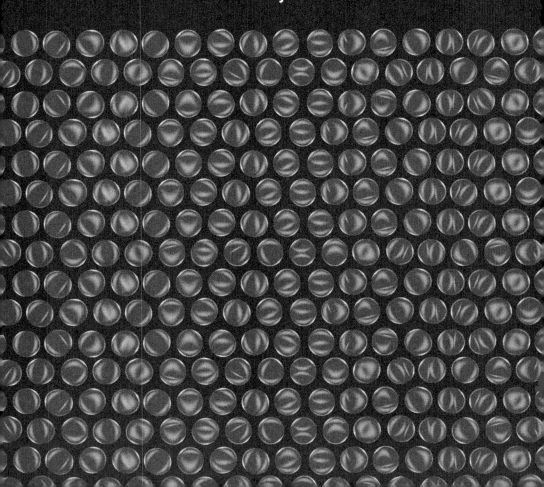

Have you ever thought about how much self-control it would take to work at a bubble-wrap factory? I know that anytime I see a piece of bubble wrap, I feel obligated to pop at least one of the bubbles.

Bubble wrap has been around as a packaging agent since 1960. Fred Bowers, a marketer at IBM, had a lot of fragile computer parts to ship in 1960, and he realized that the bubbles made a great cushion. Not only were the bubbles effective as a cushioning agent, but the bubbles also weighed almost nothing. Fred didn't know it at first, but when his customers received their computer parts, they perceived they received a bonus – a sheet of bubbles they could pop. Fred's customers loved the product as insulation, but they also liked it as a toy, and they were inclined to order more products from Fred just to get more bubbles.

Bubble wrap was created in 1957 by two Sealed Air engineers, Alfred Fielding and Marc Chavannes. They did not envision it being used as a shipping agent; they thought they had created a unique wallpaper. Hanging bamboo strips to create doors was the fad for youth in the 1950s, and they thought that strips of plastic coated with sealed bubbles could be the next big thing in home decorating in the 1960s. Alfred and Marc believed in the idea so much, they created two shower curtains with their bubble strips for the Sealed Air board to see. To their amazement – and disappointment, the board rejected their idea of a three-dimensional (3-D) textured wallpaper.

Alfred and Marc kept brainstorming possible uses for strips of bubbles of sealed air. Their second idea also envisioned the sealed air bubbles as wall covering, but this time it was for practical purposes rather than decorative purposes. They had noticed that their sealed bubbles on plastic strips would allow the sun to come through while providing some insulation from cold outdoor weather, so they decided to appeal to greenhouses to install the strips of bubbles as insulation to protect plants. Alfred and Marc went to the Sealed Air board again, and this time the board agreed to let Alfred and Marc market their product to greenhouses. Although Alfred and Marc were able to sell the idea to the board, they were not able to sell the idea to greenhouse owners; greenhouse owners were not interested in their product.

Determined that the strips of bubbles of sealed air must have some kind of use, Alfred and Marc kept looking for a market. They had noticed that the bubbles on the shower curtain they had made had a bounce to them; that is, they could hold weight and not break. What if strips of bubbles were used as insulation in shipping? They received permission from Sealed Air to see if anyone would be interested in using their product in this way. One of their contacts was Fred Bowers at IBM - and the rest is history.

Bubble wrap brings out the kid in all of us - who can resist popping a bubble or two when presented with a piece of bubble wrap? Alfred and Marc came up with three uses for Bubble wrap; today, home hacks offer numerous uses for this product Sealed Air once deemed as worthless. In fact, Bubble wrap has come full circle - I saw someone inject various colors of dye into the circles, creating a unique 3-D textured colored wallpaper. The wallpaper was - pardon the pun - to dye for.

CHAPTER 14

WOULD YOU BELIEVE...

NEW ZEALAND HAS A NATIONAL WIZARD?

"Nobody knows what the future is except for wizards."
- Gillian Jacobs

We're off to see the Wizard
The wonderful Wizard of Oz
We hear he is a whiz of a wiz
If ever a wiz there was.

Remember that song from the movie/Broadway musical *The Wizard of Oz*? Dorothy, Toto, the scarecrow, the tinman, and the lion all wanted to go see the wizard, and they knew that by following the yellow brick road, they could get there. They may have known where to find a wizard, but do you have any idea of where you and I can go to see a government-certified wizard? I do.

Lots of people may profess to be a wizard, but only one country in the world has a national wizard, so, if you want to meet an official, government-sanctioned wizard, we will have to go to New Zealand. The wizard in New Zealand may/may not be a real wizard - remember that the wizard in the Wizard of Oz was just a man behind a curtain. However, just like the wizard was to Oz, the national wizard in New Zealand is a tourist attraction.

Ian Brackenbury Channell, the current holder of the office of Wizard, has been a self-professed wizard for over forty years. Prior to moving to Australia in the 1970s, he served in the Royal Air Force and then had a position teaching English literature. He worked as a community arts organizer and a sociology instructor at a university when he came to Australia, but that job dried up. On a quest to revive school spirit (and secure employment for himself), he talked the administration into appointing him as a wizard, a role that he perceived very similar to the court jester in ancient kings' courts, someone who spoke the truth and provided wise counsel but who was also fun to have around.

His wife and university friends didn't approve of the move, and she and they went their separate ways. He was dedicated to taking on the role of wizard, however, and had no desire to go back to traditional teaching. He moved to Christchurch, one of the largest towns in New Zealand, where he made appearances at the town center in a black pointed hat and wizard garb; he also showed up as John the Baptist in a loincloth. He would stand on the square in his outfit of the day, praising some things, such as the British Empire, while railing against others, such as anti-male sexism. In time, he put aside the other costumes and settled on the identity of the wizard.

The Christchurch authorities found him to be a public nuisance but not a physical threat to anyone; the local citizens loved him. People would flock downtown just to get a glimpse of him in his wizard outfit; he became a tourist attraction. As he became more popular, authorities started to see his tourism draw and became less antagonistic towards him. Ian pushed the limits of the law but was careful not to break rules. His ways of evading the rules were humorous and memorable; for instance, when he was told he could not speak out in English, he resorted to French. (The man knows five languages.) By 1982, he was considered living art.

As he grew into the role of wizard, he may also have developed magical powers. In 1988, he beat a drum in the drought-stricken town of Waimate, a neighbor of Christchurch, and, a few hours later, rain was falling. That same year, the Christchurch City Council agreed to pay him $10,400 annually for "wizardry", and he has held the position ever since. His duties include promoting local events and welcoming dignitaries and groups into town but do not require any spells or magic from him. As a wizard, he has won the Queen's Service Award, one of the highest awards one can earn in Australia.

Men, do you think it would be fun to be a wizard? I think there is a little wizard in all of us. I don't know about you, but ladies say that I am a wizard under the sheets.

CHAPTER 15

WOULD YOU BELIEVE . . .

A BURGLAR OUTFOXED THE BUCKINGHAM PALACE SECURITY SYSTEM IN 1982 – TWICE?

"I went to Buckingham Palace and I wanted to take something from there, but there was nothing good to steal, although I did nick some serviettes with ER and Her Majesty on them from the Jubilee celebrations."
- Konnie Huq

Have you ever done something and gotten away with it - and then felt guilty? Did getting away with it haunt you? Did you feel like you ought to turn yourself in? I have heard of people who cheated on their income taxes and later sent the money they owed because the guilt got to them. (I've also heard the story of one guy who was plagued by guilt and sent half of what he owed, saying that if he still felt guilty a few days later, he would send the rest.)

Michael Fagan, a house painter turned burglar, experienced that kind of guilt. He broke into Buckingham Palace and got away with it. Breaking into Buckingham Palace is not something the average person does. Buckingham Palace is noted for its security, and the palace security has been praised in articles and poetry. For instance, do you remember A.A. Milne's poem, "Buckingham Palace?" You likely read it as a child. Here are some lines to jog your memory:

They're changing guard at Buckingham Palace -
Christopher Robin went down with Alice.
Alice is marrying one of the guard.
"A soldier's life is terrible hard,"

Says Alice.

(Milne, of course, is the British author who is famous for his stories of the teddy bear Winnie the Pooh and the boy Christopher Robin.) Although Buckingham Palace has always been known for its security, Michael thoroughly embarrassed its personnel. Michael not only broke into Buckingham Palace twice, on his second visit, he was able to successfully enter the queen's bedroom where the queen was resting. Luckily, he was a burglar, not an assassin or a rapist, for he had her cornered.

Michael used the same method to break into the palace both times - he scaled the palace gates, shimmied up a drainpipe, and then entered through a window. Michael wasn't thinking about outfoxing the security, about stealing anything, or about hurting anyone that first break-in; he was simply hoping to get an audience with the queen, Queen Elizabeth II. Michael was feeling down because his wife had left him with four kids, and he had decided to go to the queen for help. Most people do not think about going to the queen with this type of domestic problem, but he sincerely believed the queen would want to help him, one of her loyal subjects, through the situation. Due to his emotional state - as well as to liquor and drugs, he was not thinking rationally, and believed if he could just tell the queen about his situation, she would help. He knew the palace guards were not going to give him an audience with the queen; therefore, he concluded that breaking into the palace was the only alternative he had.

He was almost caught. A maid saw him as he shimmied the drainpipe, and she called security; security, though, thought she had just spooked herself. Michael had no idea he had been seen. He finished shimmying up the drainpipe and entered through an unlocked window. Finding himself alone in the palace, he helped himself to some cheddar cheese and crackers. He then took a bottle of white wine and began to nurse it as he wandered around the palace. He viewed royal portraits and even sat on a throne. Unknown to him, he tripped two alarms, but security believed the alarms were just faulty and turned them off without investigating. After not seeing the queen within the first half hour, he figured he wasn't going to be successful finding her, so he left, exiting the same way he had entered.

On July 9, he broke into the palace again, using the same route as before. A silent alarm went off, but again security personnel turned it off thinking the sensor had gone off by mistake. Michael walked the halls again and accidently knocked over a glass ashtray, cutting his hand. He was still nursing his hand and holding broken glass when he found the apartment wing of the palace; this time he found the queen's bedroom – and through the sheet-like canopy that hung around the bed, he could see the queen was lying in her bed. He gently pulled back the canopy, trying not to startle her. The queen was awake; she sat up upon seeing him and asked, "Why are you here?"

Fagan didn't answer. The queen kept her cool and stepped out into the hall to find someone to escort Fagan out of her room. Fagan let her go, admiring her tiny bare feet as she left the room. She went to a nearby phone and called the palace operator, asking that police be dispatched to her room. Six minutes passed without an officer in sight – she and Michael may have talked at that time, but no one knows for sure what was said if they did. After six minutes, the queen saw a maid in the hall, and she called the maid to join them. After a brief introduction the maid welcomed Fagan to the palace and took him to the pantry for a cigarette.

While they were in the pantry, the queen's footman who had been walking the queen's dogs joined them. The footman and Michael shared Scotch as they waited for the police to show. No one had told Michael the police were coming, but he knew they were and that everyone was stalling for them to arrive; however, Michael made no attempt to get away. You see, he felt so guilty for having broken into the palace and gotten away the first time, he had broken in again and with the intention of making sure he was caught.

Security did come and take Michael away. When things got sorted out, Michael agreed to a psychiatric evaluation and was not charged with a crime. (Michael did have to do time later for unrelated charges; he got in a fight with a police officer which resulted in three months, and he was conspiring to sell heroin, which cost him four years.) Oh, before I forget, in case you are wondering, he and his wife got back together.

CHAPTER 16

WOULD YOU BELIEVE...

A WORM CHARMER CHARMED 567 WORMS OUT OF THE GROUND IN LESS THAN 30 MINUTES?

"I don't want to stir up a can of worms."
- Alan Brazil

The United Kingdom is home to some of the goofiest - at least from my point of view - sports in the world. Did you realize it hosts the World Snail Racing Championship, World Champion Hen Racing, an annual Shrove Tuesday flipping pancake race, the toe wrestling championship, the Tin Bathtub Championship race, and bicycle polo. Most of these events are well established; the pancake race goes back to 1445. The weirdest contest of all, though, may be worm charming.

Prior to reading this sensational headline, I had never heard of worm charming. (I guess I lead a very sheltered life.) I had heard of snake charming, an event in which a person uses a horn to hypnotize a snake. I had also gone digging for worms to use as fishing bait, but I caught nowhere near 567 worms in thirty minutes and I used a shovel to dig them up - I was a brute, and there wasn't any charm about it.

Worm charming was something people did for fun prior to 1980, but since the early 1980s, worm charming has become a competitive sport. In fact, two annual Worm Charming contests are held in the United Kingdom each year. The original contest, the International Festival of Worm Charming, is held in Blackawton, south Devon, each year in May. Contestants use a wide variety of means to bring the worms to the surface - including urination. In fact, bringing worms up by urination is how the contest got started. (On that day, a man had too much to drink and took a pee in the grass. The pee hitting the dirt sounded like rain to the worms, who rose up to refresh themselves in the, uh, rain. Contestants can drink whatever liquid they want, and then spray it over the grass. As with any contest, people are always looking for an edge, so different concoctions have been tried; I think it is just a good excuse to drink beer, but, as I said earlier, I am a bit of a brute.)

The contestants work in groups of three and have fifteen minutes to find as many worms as they can in their randomly assigned plot. Each team consists of a charmer who persuades the worms to rise to the surface, a picker who snags the worm when it pokes its head above ground, and a counter who puts the worm away for safekeeping. Although urination is used by several contestants to charm the worms to the surface, most people put a fork in the ground and then "twang" it; the vibrations bring the worms to the surface. Others mimic the tap on the soil that birds do with their feet; still others try to recreate the vibrations that moles make as they tunnel the earth looking for worm prey. Whether it is to get a reward, such as a nice rain shower, or to avoid a punishment, such as a mole eating it, in all cases, the vibrations on the soil inspire the worm to come to the surface

The other contest, the World Worm Charming Championship, is held in Willaston, near Nantwich, Cheshire. Each contest is randomly assigned a piece of ground, and then they collect as many worms as they can from that ground in 30 minutes. The record is 567 worms; that's almost 19 worms per minute. The World Worm Charming Championship is significantly different in three ways - it does not allow urination, runs twice as long, and is an individual sport.

As with any sport, some people try to cheat. Although the field is a "secret," in reality, the same fields are used year after year as the festivals are located in the same place year after year. Therefore, if a person knows where in the field that they are likely to be digging, they may sow that part of the field with worms before the contest. (Yes, there is a black market for worms in the United Kingdom.)

Worm charming has the elements of physical prowess, strategic thinking, and luck. To win, a person must be in shape. Worms pop up and disappear fast - it's a life-size game of whack-a-mole - and those with slow reflexes, who are out of shape, or who have trouble bending over are going to struggle. Strategy includes studying the paddling a bird does with its feet so it can be closely mimicked, learning how to use one's urine or tuning fork so that it sounds like rain, and keeping wandering worms from going into someone else's square. There really is an art to charming - some people are great at it and most people are not.

Are you tempted to snicker at the concept of worm charming? I wouldn't do that. I for one am delighted to hear that there are people who have taken time to study worm charming. I know that global warming is already a problem, and, if Charles Darwin and the evolutionists are right, global warming will likely be a problem in the future too. Although birds and fish prey on worms, worms get their revenge by preying on dead birds and other forms of life. If the worm population explodes and global worming ever becomes a problem, worm charmers will be the Pied Pipers who save us.

CHAPTER 17

WOULD YOU BELIEVE . . .

A BEAR CARRIED LIVE AMMUNITION FOR POLISH TROOPS IN WORLD WAR II?

"Man is a tool-using animal.
Without tools he is nothing, with tools he is all."
- Thomas Carlyle

Do you have a pet? Does it do tricks? I have a pet dog, Elsa, and she won't do any tricks no matter how much I coax her. (I take that back; she does do one thing - If she believes a guest has overstayed their welcome, she will poop in front of them; it is hilarious to watch guests wrinkle their nose as she does her business, but, hey, they get the hint - especially if I am slow about cleaning it up.) Some people's dogs supposedly can perform a lot of tricks. I've met people who brag that their dogs can fetch slippers, bring newspapers, and rollover on command. This sounds impressive until you realize that other people have trained their four-legged friend to drink beer, smoke cigarettes, turn on the shower, and carry live ammunition.

At the beginning of World War II, Russia and Germany invaded Poland. Russia captured a lot of Polish troops, troops that Europe needed to defend against the Nazis, so, when Russia joined the Allies in World War II, Russia agreed these Polish prisoners could join the Allies on the Western front.

To get to the Western front from their prison, the Poles had to cross Iran. In Iran, they came across a bear cub whose parents had been killed as armies battled around them. Having pity on the cub, the Polish soldiers took it and nursed it, giving it condensed milk from a vodka bottle. They named it Wojtek and took it with them on their journey through Egypt to Italy.

As the bear grew, the soldiers taught it how to drink beer - it would drink the bottle dry and then look at it to see why more liquid wasn't coming, and how to smoke cigarettes - it would actually take a puff before swallowing the cigarette. (Cigarettes are bad for you - and for bears, and the coroner thought the cigarettes eventually caused the bear's death.) The bear learned how to turn on the shower and actually enjoyed taking a shower; in fact, the bear liked them so much that he often used all of the camp's water rations. (Talk about seeing some bear butt in the shower!)

Wojtek may have had fun, but he had to work too. The soldiers helped him fill out the necessary paperwork, and he was given a place in the army - doing so justified a ration of food for him and money to cover his transportation. He was given the rank of private, just as most people are when they join the army. Wojtek engaged in military training - he put in as many hours as the men; when the men threw an orange practicing as if it were a grenade, Wojtek would retrieve- and often eat - the orange. Wojtek received no special sleeping arrangements he spent the nights in a tent just like the soldiers.

At the Battle of Monte Cassino in Italy, the Polish Army were unable to load its cannons fast enough. All hands pitched in - correction, all hands, and paws. Soldiers swear they saw Wojtek with crates and shells of live ammunition bringing them to the soldiers; when Wojtek saw the soldiers loading cases of ammunition on to the trucks, he stood up and loaded them too - he could do the work of four men. (Skeptics say he was just playing with empty cases and shells - believe what you want. At the very least, Wotjek's antics were a morale booster.) The Polish army believed the story, and, for his heroics, Wotjek got promoted from private to corporal.

After the war, the question arose of who should keep Wotjetk. It was agreed that his army days should be over. It was also agreed that he should not go back to Poland, for the Soviet Union was in the process of making Poland a U.S.S.R. satellite, and the Polish nationalists feared Wotjek would likely be a communist mascot. Eventually, the men decided he would go to Scotland where the soldiers who had trained them for the Western front had lived.

Wotjek lived 17 years in Scotland; he had a great time in Scotland. He played soccer, attended children's birthday parties, and just relaxed being Wotjek. He died in 1963 at the Edinburgh, Scotland Zoo at the age of 21, which is the lower end for a typical lifespan of a bear. (If he just hadn't smoked . . .) Edinburgh has a statue to honor his memory.

I've said that my spouse is a bear in the morning, and Wotjek proves the metaphor is perfect. She growls a lot - a whole lot; a whole, whole lot - and she uses all the hot water in the showers, but should I find myself in trouble, she will be right there by my side. Is your spouse part bear too?

CHAPTER 18

WOULD YOU BELIEVE . . .

TOE WRESTLING IS A REAL SPORT AND AN INTERNATIONAL CHAMPION IS SELECTED EACH YEAR?

"It's a pleasant thing to be young, and have ten toes."
- Robert Louis Stevenson

This little piggy went to market,
This little piggy stayed home.
This little piggy had roast beef,
And this little piggy had none.
This little piggy became a toe wrestler . . .

Toe wrestler? That's right. Toe wrestler.

      If you have a big toe, and most people have two of them, then you have a potential toe wrestler - maybe even a champion - on your hands - er, on your foot. Who knows, the future world champion may be hiding in one of your shoes at this very moment.

Toe wrestling is a serious sport. A very, very serious sport, according to its ardent fans. Toe wrestling is a sport of both brains and brawn. Toe wrestling involves physical wrestling, but, as the name implies, it is just the toe and the foot that get to have physical contact with the opponent. The toe has got to be able to put down the other person's toe or push their foot out of the arena. The die-hard contestant can do toe exercises throughout the year to get in shape; if you recall from your human anatomy unit in biology class, there are muscles in the big toe and foot that can be developed. Toe wrestling also involves strategy; psyching out your opponent and knowing when to strike are essential.

Toe wrestling is not an Olympic Sport - at least not yet, but there is an international championship held each year in Derbyshire, United Kingdom; it has been held each year since 1976. Just as basketball originated in the United States, modern toe wrestling originated in England. Fans come for miles to watch the championship, and contestants come from throughout the world. As you might suspect, the toe wrestling champion has usually been from the United Kingdom, but Canada proved as early as 1979 that the United Kingdom did not have a monopoly on strong toes.

The rules of toe wrestling are very similar to the rules of arm wrestling or thumb wrestling. The two opponents go toe to toe (literally), lock their toes, and then try to push the other person's foot to the side so that it falls beyond the "in" line. Each tournament round consists of a series of two to three games; the first person to win two games advances to the next round. Contestants work their way through the tournament bracket until they reach the championship.

Although toe wrestling is a sport that all ages and genders can participate in, not all toes qualify. Judges check all toes wishing to compete to see if they have fungus, injuries and - believe it or not - hidden weapons. Although toe wrestling is not a blood sport, injuries do occur - toes are broken (by accident) in the competition. Some people do play very rough, especially in the early rounds, so as to intimidate future challengers - I told you that toe wrestling is both a psychological and a physical game.

Because men's toes are often bigger than women's toes and children's toes are smaller than adult's toes, toe wrestling competitions are usually broken into divisions - men, women, youth, and children. All ages can compete in toe wrestling. Toe wrestling can be enjoyed in your own house with your family and friends, and, on those nights where you feel like getting physical, there is nothing wrong with a man and a woman toe wrestling if both consent to it.

Once you experience toe wrestling, you may like it so much that you create a local club. Also, once you see it done, you may want to see it again and again. You can start with family and friends or, for those closet toe wrestlers who don't want their family to know of their love of toe wrestling- what happens at toe wrestling stays at toe wrestling, you can advertise on Craig's List or another community-wide medium to find like-minded people. Perhaps your club can even fund the club champion going to Derbyshire to the nationals; when all is said and done, your club may have the world champion in it.

Are you toe-tally ready to wrestle?

CHAPTER 19

WOULD YOU BELIEVE...

AN AMERICAN CON MAN SOLD THE EIFFEL TOWER...TWICE?

"Every time I look at the Eiffel Tower,
it completely blows my mind."
– Brian Fallon

Have you ever been embarrassed by something you have done, so embarrassed that you never told anyone about it? If you have, you can relate to Andre Poisson, the owner of a Paris scrap iron company.

Andre was one of five people invited by Count Victor Lustig to come to a hotel to hear a presentation about turning the Eiffel Tower into scrap metal. The other four people being wined- and-dined by Victor were also scrap metal dealers. What none of them realized is that Count Victor Lustig - if that was his real name - was a con artist who was running a con on them.

Victor had pulled off lots of cons, but selling the Eiffel Tower was one he nor anyone else had ever tried. Victor had thought of the idea in May 1925 while reading a newspaper story in which the reporter wrote that one day the Eiffel Tower might have to be sold for scrap metal. It was a trivial fact buried at the bottom of a story, but that fact was the seed of the con. When the reporter stated that the Eiffel Tower might have to be sold for scrap metal, the reporter was referring to an event that was years – maybe even centuries – away. Victor, though, realized that it could also be today.

Even though he did not own the Eiffel Tower, Victor believed he could sell the Eiffel Tower for scrap metal and get out of town with the money before anyone realized he had pulled a con. To pull off the con, Victor needed government letterhead. Rather than steal some, Victor found a printer who would print his name - he called himself the Deputy Director General of the Ministre de Postes et Telegraphes - on forged official letterhead. Once the letterhead was printed, he used it to send individual letters to five scrap iron executives, inviting them to a dinner at the hotel to discuss "an urgent matter".

After letting his guests dine lavishly at his expense, Lustig began his presentation explaining why the Eiffel Tower was for sale. He pointed out that the tower was only supposed to have been a temporary structure, a gateway to the 1889 World's Fair, and that it was not built to stand for even a decade; 35 years later, though, it was still standing. He stated that for political reasons, the general public could not know how unsafe it was but assured the iron dealers that the city had determined the tower badly needed repairs - repairs too expensive to perform. Therefore, the city was going to sell the tower as scrap metal - all 70,000 tons of it, and the five iron men had been called to this meeting to see if they would like to submit a bid for the tower.

All five dealers believed him and submitted bids. Victor, though, didn't look at the bids; he had already chosen Andre as his mark. Once he received Andre's bid, he wrote back, thinly disguising a request for a bribe; he stated he was a public servant who was supposed to dress well but who only received a meager salary. Andre sent the money, believing the contract for disposal of the tower would be his.

Victor accepted the bribe and got out of town, leaving Andre fuming. Andre, though, could not go to the police without confessing that he had knowingly tried to bribe what he thought was a public officer. Just as Victor had suspected, Andre was quite willing to engage in bribery but was too embarrassed to go to the police. Just to be sure Andre didn't report him, Victor read the paper each day to see if the story of the con appeared in it. Finally, after six months had passed, Victor concluded Andre was not going to report it.

Criminals are often done in by greed, and Victor, who had pulled off the perfect con and emerged very wealthy, was no exception. Since the selling of the Eiffel Tower con had worked perfectly the first time, Victor decided to pull it again. The only difference was that he used five different scrap metal executives.

These men, too, fell for Victor's tale of how the Eiffel Tower was going to have to come down, and they too placed bids. As he had done before, Victor had chosen a mark, but this time he miscalculated - the person he requested a bribe from went to the police rather than send the bribe. Upon seeing the story in the newspaper, he fled France and went to New York. He continued to con people in the United States, sometimes selecting victims most people would not dare to cross, such as the gangster Al Capone and Texas law officials. He conned for another eleven years, before finally being caught. Some of his crimes were as elaborate as the Eiffel Tower con, and he became a wanted man. In fact, the United States considered him to be an enemy of the state because he was so good at forgeries that the U.S. Treasury was worried that he could inflate the value of the dollar by putting excessive money into the system. He was eventually caught and put into Alcatraz Prison, a place he was unable to con his way out of - although he used his best charisma and tried many times by faking illness. One time, though, he was not faking the illness - that may have been the only time in his entire life when he was telling the full truth.

Count Victor Lustig, if he really was a Count - he had at least 56 known aliases, many of which had in-depth background stories, but not even one - even the one he repeated over and over about his childhood in Austria - checked out. Victor was one of the world's greatest - if not the greatest, conman in history.

I find it ironic that his most famous con was the selling of the Eiffel Tower. Did you ever stop to think that he and the Eiffel Tower are very much alike in name? The Eiffel Tower is a Paris site, and he was a parasite.

CHAPTER 20

WOULD YOU BELIEVE . . .

ANNE BONNY, HISTORY'S DEADLIEST FEMALE PIRATE, DISAPPEARED WITHOUT A TRACE?

"As to hanging, it is no great hardship. For were it not for that,
every cowardly fellow would turn pirate and so unfit the sea,
that men of courage must starve."
– Anne Bonny.

When you think of a pirate, what pops into your mind? A man with a hook? A man with a peg leg? An outlaw who hijacked ships? A thug who demanded toll fees to let ships pass without destroying them? A patriot who fought for his country but did it his way instead of following strict military guidelines? A treasure seeker? An adventurer who wanted to see distant lands?

What probably doesn't pop into mind is a woman. There were women pirates, though. Some of these women even had their own fleet of ships and were in charge of the crew. Female pirates could be found throughout the world - Grace O'Malley was off the coast of Ireland, Ching Shih was in the South China Sea, and Anne Bonny was in the Caribbean.

Anne wasn't the only female pirate in the Caribbean, but she is the most famous and most ruthless. Anne, a fiery redhead with a temper to match, grew up in Ireland in a dysfunctional middle-class family. Her dad had an affair with the maid, and, when his wife threw him out, he tried to take Anne with him. He disguised her as a boy and called her "Andy". Although her dad chose a boy for her to marry, she fell for John Bonny, a pirate with nothing to his name. When Anne refused to marry the man her dad wanted, he threw her out.

Anne moved from Ireland to the Bahamas to be with her pirate husband. The Bonny marriage, though, turned sour when her husband agreed to be a secret informant for the governor, telling the governor about the movements of pirates so the governor could arrest them. One time, her husband believed twenty-year-old Anne had been seeing other men and he charged her with adultery and ordered her whipped in public. John "Calico Jack" Rackham, a reformed pirate, had offered to give her husband money to spare the whipping, but he refused to take it. Calico Jack then convinced Anne to run away with him and become a pirate. In a daring move, they stole a ship, and headed out to sea, their fates tied together. Calico Jack returned to what he did best - pirating, and Anne was at his side.

Anne was not the only pirate sailing with Calico Jack; so was another famous female pirate, Mary Reed. In her youth, Mary had disguised herself as a boy - she called herself "Mark" - and had got a job on a British man-of-war. On the ship she ultimately revealed her true gender to the captain; they had fallen in love, settled down in the Netherlands, and operated a tavern, the Three Horseshoes. When her husband died, Mary sold the tavern and returned to sailing life. Disguised as Mark, she took a ship to the West Indies in search of adventure. The ship she was on, though, was captured by Calico Jack. Unaware that Mary was a woman, Jack offered her and other crew members the opportunity to join him as a pirate rather than face death. Mary agreed.

As they sailed, Mary revealed her gender to Anne, and the two became great friends. From time to time, Mary and Anne wore traditional women's clothing around the sailors, but, when prepared for battle, they always dressed in men's fashion. When called upon to fight, the two women would stand back-to-back, each holding a pistol in one hand and a machete in the other. They literally had each other's back.

For two months in 1720, Jack, Anne, and Mary ruled the seas, and their fame spread far and wide. (You may not realize it, but they are all recalled in modern culture; for instance, Jack flew a black flag with a skull and two criss-crossing sabers imprinted in white on it, and that is the stereotyped pirate flag used in movies such as *Pirates of the Caribbean*.) A bounty was on Calico Jack's head, so both other pirates and government officials sailed the seas hoping to capture him.

One evening after Calico Jack had captured a large Spanish ship, his crew was celebrating with alcohol and were so intoxicated that the crew of a British government ship was able to come aboard his ship unannounced. Most of Jack's men were in the ship's galley and immediately surrendered. Anne and Mary, who were upstairs relaxing with Jack in the captain's quarters, fought until they were clearly overwhelmed. All the pirates were taken to prison and most sentenced to death. Anne snarled in frustration as the men were led past her, "If you had just fought like men, you wouldn't be hanging like dogs." Anne and Mary, though, both escaped the death penalty – but not prison – because they were pregnant. Anne was found to be carrying Jack's baby and Mary was carrying a crew member's child. Mary got a fever and died in prison, but no one knows what happened to Anne.

Anne may have died around the same time, but it is more likely she made it to Charleston, South Carolina, where she quietly lived out the rest of her days; most scholars believe that she lived until 1782. This theory is backed by three facts. One, her husband John still worked for the governor and had followed her career closely - in fact, he had told the governor about her whereabouts; it is quite possible that he arranged for her freedom. Two, her father had become a very wealthy man and he may have bribed officials to let her go free. Three, Anne was raised in a middle-class home and knew how to fit in with the middle class; the presence of a baby likely brought an end to her pirating days.

No one knows for sure where the physical body of Anne went, but her spirit is alive today. Although many would object to her lifestyle, most recognize her as a leader in the women's rights movement. She receives praise for standing up to her dad when he suggested whom she should marry; she demonstrated that men should not dictate a woman's future. She is also praised for daring to be a pirate; she did not allow gender to be a barrier to having the career that she wanted. She also receives accolades for being able to handle a sword, gun, and machete as well or better than most of the men on Jack's boat; she was proof that women were not frail, delicate, and in need of a man's protection. Perhaps more than any other pirate, Anne continues to influence modern culture - and that's the way things arrrrrrrrrr!

CHAPTER 21

WOULD YOU BELIEVE...

THE GAME MONOPOLY WAS INTENDED TO RADICALIZE PLAYERS TO CREATE GREAT CHANGES IN SOCIETY?

"Competition is always a good thing. It forces us to do our best.
A monopoly renders people complacent and satisfied with mediocrity."
- Nancy Pearcey

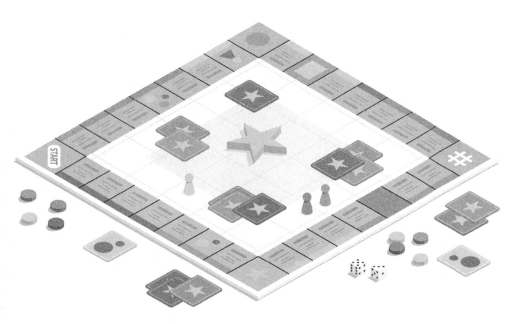

I don't know about you, but I have had some wild and crazy nights. Believe it or not, this past week I spent some time in jail. Yes, jail. The nice thing about jail is that you get to stay for free and, although you can't do any work, your investment income continues to pay you money. My friends dropped by to visit and told me that inflation was getting out of control. When I got out of jail, I drove my car to a hotel; as soon as I saw the prices, I knew I would have to file for bankruptcy. It was not my greatest week.

Do your Monopoly game nights go like that too? Believe it or not, the board game Monopoly was designed by Lizzie Maggie in 1904 as a teaching tool about monopolies and inflation. (I hate it when I think I am just having fun and, come to find out, I am learning something.) She called it The Landlord's Game, and it is very similar to the version Parker Brothers have today - it had railroads, a jail, property to build on, a "go to jail" and a "go" with rules similar to today's rules. The game was distributed in the early 1900s by a New York publisher.

Money was tight for most people in the early 1900s, so many people created a homemade version of The Landlord's Game. Charles Darrow likely saw people playing versions, but he claimed the concept as his own and sold the concept to Parker Brothers in 1935. Parker Brothers found out about Lizzy, and they offered her $500 - $9683.27 in today's money, a nice sum but not nearly enough to quit one's job to enjoy a life of luxury - for the rights to the game. Lizzie accepted, thinking her message was going to reach the masses. Since 1935 Monopoly has sold 270 million copies; been played by approximately 1 billion people, distributed in 43 languages, and sold in 111 countries. The game continues to be very popular; my family played an electronic video game version on the television set last week. A lot more Monopoly games are started than finished, but most people in today's culture recognize the land deed cards and the top-hat wearing mascot, Rich Uncle Milburn Pennybags, who is nicknamed "Mr. Monopoly".

Lizzie was a feminist, but she lived in the era before women could vote. She was strongly opinionated, though, and she wanted to educate people about the danger of - get this - monopolies. She believed that people like John D. Rockefeller and Andrew Carnegie - people who had so much money that they didn't know what to do with it - were the reason that so many common citizens were poor or struggling. She believed monopolies were an evil and believed that if people experienced becoming bankrupt by a monopoly, they would come to that same realization.

When Lizzie sold her patent to Parker Brothers in 1935, she was thrilled that her teaching tool was going to be reaching thousands of people. Parker Brothers sales did not disappoint her. Parker Brothers sold 278,000 copies the first year and 1,750,000 copies the next year. However, Lizzie's anti-monopoly message did not get out as she intended for it to. Instead of teaching people to despise monopolies as she hoped it would, it taught people to crave monopolies. To make matters worse, Parker Brothers chose to ignore her educational purpose of the game. Even more devastating for her, instead of just ignoring the anti-monopoly teaching she desired, Parker Brothers deliberately tried to keep people from finding the original purpose - they shared Charles's story as the inspiration for the game with the public and never told the public about her role.

Some things just can't be covered up indefinitely, though, and eventually the truth has seeped out. The issues of a small handful of people having the majority of the money – and with it most of the power - still plague the nation. The government has tried to break up monopolies such as AT&T, but the pieces keep merging, and fewer and fewer competitors are there to compete with AT&T. Conglomerates often own multiple brands; many people often don't realize the products they buy are all under the same company. (Did you know that Marlboro cigarettes is owned by the same company that owns Oreo Cookies or that Pizza Hut and Mountain Dew are owned by the same company?) If you aren't afraid to bring out your rebel side, the next time you pass go and collect $200, pause to think about the issues Lizzie intended for you to think about as you play the game. When you are down to your final $100, be glad it's just a game, but be angered that the world we live in is - at least according to Lizzie - going to bankrupt us in real life unless we stop the monopolies.

CHAPTER 22

WOULD YOU BELIEVE . . .

THE U.S.S.R. WANTED TO DROP NUCLEAR BOMBS ON ITSELF - AND DAM THE PACIFIC OCEAN?

"In nuclear war all men are cremated equal."
- Dexter Gordon

I used to live in northern Illinois, a place where it is possible to experience all four seasons of the year in one day. When people said, "If you don't like the weather, just wait for a couple of hours," they meant it. While I was in college, I used to wake up at four o'clock to be at my fast-food job at five o'clock. At 4:30 a.m. when I left the house, it was below freezing outside. By the time I got done with my shift at 1 p.m., it was in the 70s or 80s outside. We had gone from winter to summer in about eight hours, and in another eight hours we would move from summer back to winter.

Needless to say, with this drastic temperature change, it was very easy to forget one's coat when one left the store in the summertime temperatures at the end of one's shift. I would usually change clothes, get my coat from my locker, and then set my coat on the back counter while I went to the cashier to take advantage of the free meal the company provided. I would then get my meal, retrieve my coat, and head to my college class.

Sometimes I would forget that "retrieve my coat" step. I was not the only one who forgot my possessions, so the manager decided to teach us a lesson. Instead of putting our coats safely in the manager's office, she took our coats and hosed them in large pans. She then took the soaking wet coats and the pans of water they were in and placed them on an empty shelf in the walk-in freezer. When I came to retrieve my coat, it was frozen like a rock. I could see my coat beneath the shell of water, but I could not get it out.

The Soviet Union faced that same type of situation after World War II, but on a much grander scale. The Soviet Union had land in Siberia and the Arctic that had great resources, but, because of the ice, almost all that people could do was look at these resources and acknowledge they were there. The resources were worthless in their current conditions, and, to generate jobs and to keep ahead of the United States in the space race, the Soviet Union needed those supplies.

Like Wylie Coyote, the Soviet Union schemed about how to break the ice and retrieve their resource. They seriously considered schemes that would drive today's climate activists insane - they considered dropping nuclear bombs to reroute rivers so the rivers would cause the ice to melt, and they considered building a dam from Russia to Alaska, blocking the Pacific Ocean from getting to the Arctic. Both were taken very, very seriously.

The first made sense because the Soviet Union had a lot of nuclear bombs that it had built but had never dropped. Rather than simply dispose of the outdated bomb, it made sense to try to salvage parts from it. (The United States had a similar dilemma, and the U.S. bombs were used to make tunnels.)

The Soviet Union realized that other nations would be affected if it were to dam the Arctic so that the Pacific could not enter, thus allowing the warmer Atlantic water to melt the polar ice. It therefore shared this idea with the United States, Japan, and other nations. Believe it or not, John F. Kennedy, who was just months before being elected the U.S. President, prepared a statement about this issue before a Presidential Debate, and in that statement he made it clear that he was in favor of exploring the matter in more detail.

The decision-making climate has not changed since the mid-1940s. Global competition, the use of the environment, short-term benefits for our own generation at the risk of long-term devastation for two or three generations away, and how to dispose of unused - thank goodness, they're unused - nuclear weapons are all still issues we face today. Science has advanced, so let's hope ideas of the late 1940s don't come back into style.

My coat eventually thawed, and I wore it through many Arctic blasts - and I never forgot it at the store again. Whenever I go to a group gathering and the team leader says, "Let's break the ice", I can't help thinking about my frozen coat and the frozen Arctic. Ice certainly needs to be broken - the resources under it are not useable otherwise - but dropping bombs and building dams are not the answer.

CHAPTER 23

WOULD YOU BELIEVE...

GREAT BRITAIN ATTEMPTED TO CARVE A WORKABLE AIRCRAFT CARRIER OUT OF AN ICEBERG?

"Have a dream, chase it down, jump over every single hurdle, and run through fire and ice to get there."
- Whitney Wolfe Herd

Which is stronger, the steel of a ship or an iceberg?

If you aren't sure, just think about the *Titanic*, the huge "unsinkable" British luxury liner that sank in the North Atlantic Ocean on April 15, 1912. When the *Titanic* ran into the iceberg, the clear winner was the iceberg.

As 1942 drew to a close the United Kingdom was losing World War II to Germany. German submarines were able to sink British merchant and military ships at will in the northern Atlantic. The German submarines roamed the North Atlantic, and the British Air Force didn't have planes with deep enough fuel tanks to reach them. The British military concluded it needed an unsinkable aircraft carrier in those waters so planes could refuel and then drive back the submarines.

A creative scientist in Great Britain, Geoffrey Pyke, suggested towing an iceberg south and using it as a landing field. The torpedoes and bombs of 1942 could not destroy ice; ice was considered an unsinkable material. Ice was also free; metal was in very short supply. This idea of towing an iceberg was not practical, however. Icebergs are typically ten percent above the water, and their pyramid shape extends far into the ocean. Finding an iceberg long enough to land planes on was not realistic to move because of how huge the amount of ice underneath it would be.

After further brainstorming, Pyke suggested building a fleet of aircraft carriers out of ice, and he laid out his plan to British Prime Minister Winston Churchill. Building materials were traditionally wood, metal, and cement, but Churchill was willing to entertain the idea of using ice. He gave permission for the prototype to be constructed.

The scientists quickly realized that carving the boat from ice and having a launching pad on top was not reasonable. However, the scientists did not give up on the idea of a ship made primarily of ice. They decided to use ice to construct the hull, and then use normal building materials around the ice to complete the ship. Churchill okayed the modified version, and work begun on it.

The ship was named *HMS Habakkuk* (or Habbakuk), a deliberate - and intentionally misspelled - reference to the Biblical prophet who proclaimed, "Look at the nations and watch - and be utterly amazed. For I am going to do something in your days that you would not believe, even if you were told" (Habakkuk 1:5). Construction on the *HMS Habakkuk* began at Lake Jaspar in Alberta, Canada in December 1942. The boat was going to be twice the size of the *Titanic*, 2000 feet long and 200 feet wide.

To keep the ice cold, engineers built a refrigeration unit around it. In essence, it was a giant ice-cube with a shell around it and pieces of boat built at each end. The ribs of the ship were refrigerator coolant.

Construction of the prototype did not go smoothly. Some piping that arrived bent could not be used, so the boat had to be engineered for air, not water, to go through the coolant system. This bad news hampered the project, but so did a lot of good news - Iceland agreed to let the United Kingdom use its land to launch planes; technology for plane building had advanced so now planes could fly greater distances without refueling; and new radar made it easier to track German submarines. By the summer of 1943, the project was scrapped, and the contents were allowed to sink into the bottom of the lake.

People around Lake Jaspar when the boat was under construction had no idea of what they were seeing being built. They nicknamed the project "Noah's Ark" after the Biblical story of a man named Noah who took two of each animal into a boat to preserve their species when a flood came upon the world. Today, if you ever go scuba diving in Lake Jaspar, you can still see remnants of the construction, and a plaque has even been placed upon them explaining their historical significance (and asking people not to steal the remains).

World War II had a lot of scientific firsts - the aircraft carrier, the long-range bomber, and the atom bomb, but the building of an aircraft carrier of ice was definitely the most chilling (literally) experiment undertaken.

CHAPTER 24

WOULD YOU BELIEVE...

RUSSIAN COSMONAUTS WERE ARMED WITH PISTOLS AND MACHETES IN OUTER SPACE?

"That's one small step for a man, one giant leap for mankind."
- Neil Armstrongipsum

Do you believe that a *Star Wars*-like battle will ever rage in outer space? I do. I look at current world history, and I believe we are moving closer to it all the time.

One reason I believe that we are is because we now have a branch of the military devoted exclusively to space. On December 20, 2019, the United States began the Space Force, the first official independent space force. Prior to that, the Air Force had a unit focused on space, but it was more of an afterthought than a primary focus.

The Space Force serves many purposes. Satellites need to be protected from people who want to do away with them, valuable minerals may be found on planets that pirates might like to steal, and questions about boundaries may arise as more nations enter the final frontier. We rely on our satellites - I do most of my research on the Internet today instead of using traditional books. The concept of having Americans armed in space - I love that Second Amendment right, don't you? - may sound foreign to the Western world, but the concept of bringing weapons into space is not new - Russian cosmonauts carried pistols and machetes into space since the earliest launches of humans into space.

You read that right - the Russian cosmonauts were armed. The early cosmonauts carried a 9 mm pistol and later ones were given a triple-barreled TP Survival Pistol. Not only could these triple-barrel guns take down large predators, but they could also fire flares. As if that were not enough, their buttstock opened to reveal a large machete that could be used to slice and dice. Cosmonauts were not civilians; they were trained soldiers

Neither 9 mm pistols nor TP Survival Pistols do much good in space, though. The air is oxygen rich, and gravity is very weak. Only a fool would shoot a triple-barreled TP-82 Survival Pistol in the vacuum of space or inside the spaceship. Luckily, the cosmonauts realized this, and never fired their weapon in space.

Although taken with them into space, the guns weren't needed for space; the guns were needed for earth. Whereas the United States used to send its returning astronauts for a splashdown in the ocean, the U.S.S.R. had its cosmonauts parachute to safety into rural Siberia. (Needless to say, spaceships were not reusable in those days.) One day in 1965, Alexei Leonov, the first person to spacewalk, and his co-cosmonaut, Pavel Belyayev, had to land in the Ural mountains, a snow-covered, forest covered area over 600 miles off their target. They had to wait in the sparsely inhabited, bear-infested forested wilderness over two days for skiers to rescue them; both credit their weapons from preventing them becoming bear-chow.

I am still waiting for my flying car that was promised by the Jetsons and others in the 1960s. Science has moved much slower than people expected, but the concept of electric, self-driving cars are now close to being a reality, and it will likely just be a matter of time - lots of time - before flying cars exist. If someone can envision it, that person may be able to turn the vision into reality. The same is true with space wars; they may be several generations away, but, unless humans destroy themselves first - space battles will be as common as ship battles were on the high seas as countries competed for the land and resources of the New World.

CHAPTER 25

WOULD YOU BELIEVE...

THE PARASUIT CAME BEFORE THE PARACHUTE?

"I got quite bored when I was hanging in the air.
I want to do it without a parachute next."
- Rhona Mitra

Have you ever played group games with a parachute? When I was a kid, both the summer camp and the school I attended had a parachute they brought out for recreation time. Everyone was to stand spaced equal-distanced around the chute and hold onto the chute. We would bounce a ball to each other by waving the chute, and we would fill the chute with air and then let it fall on us. If you have ever touched a parachute, take a moment, and recall how it feels to the touch.

If you haven't seen a parachute, have you ever seen parachute pants? Parachute pants are baggy pants with a drawstring at the waist and elastic cuffs to hold them in place. The pants are made from a lightweight nylon fabric; the material is similar in texture and weight to the material used in parachutes. Parachute pants became a fad in the 1980s and were often associated with breakdancing. People - at least the ones I have talked to - know that parachute pants are not really parachutes and that they will not save one's life if one is falling from a plane.

What about a parachute suit - known as a parasuit; would an outfit made of all parachute material plus a traditional parachute in one's backpack be able to save one's life if one was falling from an airplane? Seventy years before parachute pants came onto the scene, the parachute suit was invented. The parachute suit WAS intended to save one's life if one fell from a plane. Franz Reichelt, a French tailor came up with the idea for the suit.

In 1912, aviation was taking off. Lots of people were flying, but - machines being machines - sometimes problems would occur when the planes were in the air. The parachute was being developed by several people, including Franz Reichelt, and each person wanted to be the first to fulfill society's needs. There was a lot of money to be made because people needed the product. In 1912, if a plane went down and you were in it, you faced almost certain death.

Franz had thrown lots of dummies from the roof of his courtyard and had made the chute lighter and lighter from those experiments. His courtyard, though, was not high enough to give the parachute adequate time to open. He needed to drop it from an extreme height, such as the Eiffel Tower.

Franz had convinced Parisian authorities to let him test his parachute suit on the Eiffel Tower, and they had granted him approval to throw a dummy wearing his suit from the tower. This was not the first time the Eiffel Tower had been used for such a purpose; the previous year, Charles Broaderick had tested out his idea for a parachute from the Eiffel Tower, and his dummy had floated safely to the ground.

The Eiffel Tower also provided publicity. The concept of the parachute was new, and people flocked to see this new invention. Franz was already a renowned tailor, and hundreds of people, press, and security came to see him.

Franz's took advantage of this free advertising and strutted around in his parasuit for all to see. Franz demonstrated that his suit allowed the wearer to move around as in any other clothing; movement was not restricted. People were free to look in the back of the suit and the backpack, the place where the parachute itself was stored. The whole suit weighed 9 kilograms.

With the press and hundreds of people below, Franz climbed the dizzying heights of the Eiffel Tower. People saw Franz in his parachute suit, but they thought he was still simply modeling it. Franz had told authorities that a dummy was going to jump, but as he climbed the steps, Franz concluded that he personally would do the jump. Perhaps it was the fact that someone had parachuted off the Statue to Liberty two days earlier or perhaps it was a desire to one-up Broaderick, but Franz concluded that he – not the dummy – should do the jump.

Franz shared his plans with his friends as they continued their climb. His friends tried to talk him out of it. Seeing he was headstrong, one suggested that he at least wear safety equipment. Franz was confident in his invention, and he did not want any ropes or anything that could be construed as trickery. He refused all safety equipment except his parasuit.

Once on the first ledge, Franz looked down on the crowd 187 feet below him. People began to gasp when they saw that he was going to do the jump. He stood on the ledge 40 seconds, weighing the pros and cons; no one rushed to stop him. Like a scared swimmer doing a cannonball off the high dive, Franz summoned up his courage, committed himself to the fall, and let gravity take it from there.

His chute opened, but he was already too close to the ground. The impact killed him instantly. Needless to say, the parasuit never did catch on. Franz, though, did show the world one way that did not work, and thereby helped people to find the way that does work. Today, we take parachutes for granted. Many of my friends go skydiving just for the thrill of skydiving; but there is very little risk. The U.S. Army has units of paratroopers, people who jump from planes often behind enemy lines; their biggest risk is enemy gunfire but not the fall itself. The Flying Tailor may have failed with his parasuit, but he is greatly responsible for the parachute we have today. This tailor wasn't just any o' sew-and-sew.

CHAPTER 26

WOULD YOU BELIEVE ...

PEOPLE USED TO PAY PEOPLE TO TAP ON THEIR WINDOWS TO WAKE THEM UP?

"I set my alarm for 7:30 A.M.,
but it's really hard for me to wake up in the mornings."
- Hannah Brown

Technology is constantly replacing old jobs with new ones. A hundred years ago no one would have thought of being a computer code writer or a video game designer as a career. Two hundred years ago, no one would have thought of being a movie actress or an airplane pilot. To make way for new jobs, old ones are pushed aside. Today, we see the cashier at large stores being replaced with self-checkout; in a few years, the cashier may be as rare as the full-service gas station attendant.

Ever think about some old jobs and wonder what they were like. For instance, building a Roman chariot or even a covered wagon would be an interesting experience. How would you like to be a knocker-upper? (When I heard that read aloud, I thought it was a "knocker her up"-per, but it really is a "knocker-upper," which is completely different.)

If you enjoy nightlife and don't mind going to sleep until after the break of dawn each day, then this is perhaps your ideal job. There are slight physical requirements - you must be able to walk around a neighborhood and you must carry a pole that is long enough to tap on a second-story window.

The knocker-upper profession came into existence with the start of the industrial revolution. Because the assembly line required that each member of the shift be present, getting to work on time was essential if one wanted to hold a job. The purpose of the knocker-upper was to make sure the factory worker was awake. (I personally use a series of alarm clocks to make sure I am awake, with each clock that goes off farther from my bed so that either the sound or the walk wakes me. In the 1500s - 1940s when knocker-uppers thrived, though, alarm clocks were not common nor were they reliable or affordable.)

Early knocker-uppers would pound on the front door until someone answered, but, because this was often at 5 a.m., family members and neighbors did not appreciate it. Knocker-uppers then began to rap on the factory worker's bedroom window; the window was usually on the second floor, so that is why they used the stick. Some knocker-uppers would quit after three solid whacks, but others would keep going until the worker greeted them. (Some were enthusiastic "good mornings" and "thanks for waking me", but other greetings could not be published in this book without making it unfit for all children and most adults - let's just say people greeted the waker-upper just like you greet your alarm clock.)

To make a living as a waker-upper, you needed to have about 100 clients. Therefore, waker-uppers were usually found in factory towns and large cities. The waker-upper was prevalent especially in England and Ireland until the 1940s when alarm clocks became commonplace. The profession petered out in the 1970s. The waker-upper provided a valuable service to the community and kept the factories producing and the people employed. The waker-upper would typically go to sleep after completing the morning round and, should the waker-upper oversleep by an hour or two, all he missed was nightlife.

I prefer my alarm clock over a man tapping on my window. What I really prefer is a beautiful woman. Beautiful women know how to get me up.

CHAPTER 27

WOULD YOU BELIEVE...

RUSSIA BUGGED THE U.S. EMBASSY IN MOSCOW FOR SEVEN YEARS WITHOUT DETECTION... AND THEN WAS HUMILIATED AT THE UNITED NATIONS BY THAT VERY BUG?

"Spying has always gone on since ancient times."
- Vladimir Putin

Do you remember reading *Homer's Iliad and Odyssey* in which Homer describes how the Greeks built a wooden horse, came up to the Trojan fortress with it, and ran away? Do you recall how the Trojans couldn't decide if it was a weapon that Greeks planned to use that hadn't worked or if it was a gift to soften the Trojans because the Greeks planned to surrender? Failed weapon or a gift, the Trojans decided to bring it into their city walls. Unknown to the Trojans, though, the belly of the horse contained Greek soldiers, and, once it became night, the Greek soldiers undid the hatch and let themselves out. A couple of Greek soldiers snuck to the city gates, overcame the guards, and opened the gates so that the Greek army could get inside the city. Troy was completely surprised and surrendered shortly after that. From that story, we get the saying, "Beware of Greeks bearing gifts." That story may be truth, or it may be fiction - or some of both, but there is no doubt the Greeks won the war.

Do you believe that the United States would be silly enough to fall for a trick like that? If you answered yes, then you are correct. In 1945, the United States embassy in Moscow accepted a gift from the U.S.S.R. and it took seven years for the United States to realize the gift had a cavity in which The Thing hid and that the United States had been duped.

Children are the most innocent of all people, so the U.S. Ambassador had his guard down when Russian school children presented him with a carved, wooden seal of the United States as World War II wound down in 1945. The children said the seal was a token of the U.S.S.R.'s appreciation of America working with it in World War II. I like to think the children didn't know The Thing resided inside of it, and that they were just pawns in a sinister chess game.

The ambassador hung the Seal in the study of his residence. Little did he realize that inside the Seal was a tiny antenna, nicknamed "The Thing", that could transmit sound. The antenna did not have its own power source but relied on a van outside to turn it on and off. For six years no one even suspected a bug had been planted. The West began to become aware of The Thing's existence in 1951, when British agents picked up a conversation that they thought might be coming from the ambassador's study. In 1952, the United States became convinced the study had a bug. However, after a sweep for bugs, nothing was detected.

Realizing that the bug might have been turned off when they did their hunt for it, techs asked the current ambassador to pretend to dictate an important memo. When the "important memo" began to be dictated, the techs realized the radio signals were coming from the Seal. They looked at the Seal, but they could not find the bug on it. Convinced the Seal had somehow been fixed to relay radio signals but having no clue as to how, one agent put the Seal under his pillow overnight so that the U.S.S.R could not steal it. The next day, the Seal was sent to the United States, where it was discovered that "The Thing" was not on it – it was in it - buried in the center.

The United States studied the technology but did not let the U.S.S.R. know it had found The Thing. In 1960, when the U.S.S.R. went to the United Nations to complain that the United States had been spying on it with an airplane, the United States showed The Thing to the world. The United States did not deny it had flown over the U.S.S.R. to spy on it, but it challenged the U.S.S.R.'s accusation that it was the aggressor, for The Thing proved that the Russians had started spying on Americans before Americans started to spy on Russians.

Beware of Greeks bearing gifts; beware of Russians bearing gifts too. There is no such thing as a "free lunch;" everything comes at a price. People like to manipulate us with gifts and make us feel obligated with gifts. No one ever knows what Thing is attached to a gift!

CHAPTER 28

WOULD YOU BELIEVE...

A MUSEUM CUSTODIAN WALKED OUT WITH THE ORIGINAL *MONA LISA* UNDER HIS SHIRT?

"*Mona Lisa* is the only beauty who went through
history and retained her reputation."
- Will Rogers

Men have always had a fascination with painted women; in fact, prostitution is one of the oldest professions on record. However, not all painted women are prostitutes; there is another kind of painted woman, the woman who sits for a portrait. Although many women have sat to be painted, only one is known for her smile – the *Mona Lisa*. When Leonardo da Vinci painted the *Mona Lisa* in the early 1500s, he captured a smile that few people have ever been able to replicate. It's fitting then that when Vincenzo Peruggia stole the *v* from the Louvre on August 21, 1911, he committed a crime no one has been able to replicate since.

Da Vinci started painting the picture in 1503 and had the bulk of it done by 1506, but he was still touching it up in 1517. (As a writer, I can relate – some masterpieces are just never quite done.) The picture, an oil painting on a white Lombardy poplar panel, is likely of Lisa Gherardini, an Italian nobleman's wife. Da Vinci never provided a clue about the mysterious smile. (If you have never seen it, it will remind you of a woman with braces on her teeth who has been asked to smile but she doesn't want to show any metal. People have speculated she may have seen someone in the same outfit she was wearing or that she was sad on the day Da Vinci asked her to smile.) When invited by the French to be a part of the king's court, Da Vinci left Italy with the painting and presented it as a gift to the French king, Francis I, upon arriving in the king's court.

Vincenzo Peruggia, a twenty-first century Louvre Museum custodian with Italian roots, walked by the painting each day; the royal family had placed the painting there in 1797 so the public could enjoy it. Vincenzo seethed with rage each time he saw it. Seeing the painting reminded him that French dictator Napoleon Bonaparte had conquered Italy and had stolen many Italian masterpieces; Vincenzo likely believed the Mona Lisa was one of them. Rather than just fume, he formulated a plan to steal the Mona Lisa and return it to Italy.

What authorities say Vincenzo did and what he says that he did varies slightly, but all agree that the theft was bold and simplistic. Vincenzo either hid in the museum after his shift or walked into the museum on his day off. He wore a white smock like the museum employees wore, walked up to the painting, and removed it from the wall. He then went into a nearby stairwell and removed the frame, wrapped the painting in the smock, and exited the building.

Museum personnel noticed it was missing almost immediately, but they thought that the painting had been taken elsewhere in the museum to be restored. It wasn't until two days later that they realized that the painting had been stolen.

Vincenzo and the *Mona Lisa* may have been smiling, but the guards certainly were not as one of the greatest manhunts of the period got underway.

For the next two years, the painting may have sat in Vincenzo's apartment - notice the word "may," we're going to come back to that. After nearly two years, Vincenzo went to Italy where he tried to find a buyer - that's right, he did not just give it to an Italian museum director to hang. Although he wanted to give the painting back to the Italian people to whom he felt it belonged, he thought that he deserved a reward for returning it to Italy. His Florence contact took the painting, got it authenticated, and then promptly called the police. The painting, now more famous than ever, was displayed throughout Italy and then returned to the Louvre. Vincenzo, meanwhile, was put on trial and found guilty of theft; however, he was regarded as a patriot and a hero, and he spent only a short time in jail.

But is this really what happened? Many people question if an Italian janitor could have come up with such a scheme on his own. These people suggest that Vincenzo was a pawn of a millionaire, such as J.P. Morgan, who paid him to steal the painting and bring it to him. During those two years, the painting was given to the best artists money could buy; people who could replicate every detail so closely that it could pass the eye of the most astute critic. After the perfect forgery was finished, Vincenzo then provided the forgery to the Italian museum, causing the police to stop their investigation.

Was he truly patriotic? Was he motivated by money? Did he work alone? Is it truly the original *Mona Lisa* that hangs in the Louvre? Just as the reason for the *Mona Lisa's* smile will never be known, the answers to these questions never will be either. One thing that is for sure, though - painted women still inspire men to do things they ordinarily would never do.

CHAPTER 29

WOULD YOU BELIEVE ...

TOYMAKERS MADE THE TEDDY BEAR IN HONOR OF THE U.S. PRESIDENT, THEODORE ROOSEVELT; THEY MADE A POSSUM IN HONOR OF HIS SUCCESSOR?

"It's too bad we're not all teddy bears.
More stuffing would only make us cuter and cuddlier."
- Richelle E. Goodrich

Do you remember your Teddy Bear from your childhood? I have mine in my closet at my mom's house. In my childhood, he looked a little different - part of that is a child's memory and the other part is genuine wear and tear. I named him Beary. (Looking back, I admit that it was not the most original name.) Beary and I went on numerous adventures. With him by my side, my mom's couch became a car one day and an airplane the next. I made him clothes out of sheets of paper and Scotch tape - I even made a pair of shoes for myself. Almost every child has a Teddy Bear. If you didn't have one, you missed out on something special.

The Teddy Bear is named after Theodore "Teddy" Roosevelt, the 26th President of the United States. Theodore Roosevelt enjoyed the outdoors. One day in 1902, Theodore was wrapping up a bear hunting trip in Mississippi. Although there were bears around, Theodore had not found one. Realizing the President had not shot a bear and knowing that might make for bad headlines, one of his friends who came across a bear captured it rather than killed it. He brought the bear back to the campsite, tied it to a tree, and invited the President to shoot. Theodore said that shooting a bear that could not fight back was not sporting, and he refused to shoot the helpless bear. The press got word of this story of how Theodore had spared the bear's life. (What the press didn't tell the public is that the bear had been injured in attaching it to the tree, so, to put the bear out of its misery, one of his friends killed it.) A toy company decided to commemorate the occasion with a stuffed plush bear. They asked the President for permission to use his name, and he granted it for "Teddy's Bear". Over the years, the name morphed into "Teddy Bear".

With Theodore Roosevelt leaving the White House in 1909, toymakers anticipated that the demand for the teddy bear would drop to almost nothing. William Taft, an Ohio native, had won the 1908 election and was supposed to take office in January, so money-hungry toymakers pondered what animal they could associate with President Taft.

They didn't have to look hard; Taft was associated with the possum. This association, though, was due to the pleasantly plump President-elect liking to dine on them. The toy makers didn't care. Just as they had shortened Theodore to "Teddy" and then given the name of the animal "Bear" to create "Teddy Bear"; they shortened William to "Billy" and then gave the name of the animal "Possum" to create "Billy Possum".

The Georgia Billy Possum Company welcomed President Taft to office with a nationwide "Goodbye, Teddy Bear; Hello, Billy Possum" marketing blitz. Anticipating a high demand, thousands of Billy Possums were sent to stores, ready to be grabbed by patriotic children who wanted to be a part of the fad. However, despite the great amount of advertising, Billy didn't sell.

Billy sat in toy bins and on checkout counter shelves, just waiting for someone to take him home, but few did. President Taft was not nearly as popular as President Roosevelt, and his first year in office did not endear - or should I say, en-possum? - him to the public. Also, the backstory was lacking; President Roosevelt saving a bear brought out emotions, but President Taft eating a possum meant little. Most of all, most people had never seen a wild bear and a cute cuddly bear made sense, but they had seen a wild possum - a hissing, mean creature - and no matter how sweet Billy looked, he was still a possum. When Christmas time rolled around, Billy was removed from store shelves to make room for more popular items.

It's been over 120 years since the first Teddy Bear, and, to this day, the Teddy Bear is still king of the stuffed animal kingdom. Some, like Billy Possum, have made gallant efforts to oust the bear, but no one has succeeded. With chains like Build-a-Bear introducing the Teddy Bear to yet another generation, the Teddy Bear appears to be firmly rooted in our culture for at least another generation. Those, my friend, are the bear facts!

CHAPTER 30

WOULD YOU BELIEVE...

UP TO 400 PEOPLE DANCED THEMSELVES TO DEATH IN STRASBOURG BETWEEN JULY AND SEPTEMBER OF 1518?

"Dance, dance, dance till you drop."
- Author: W. H. Auden

Have you ever had boogie fever? Boogie fever is when the urge to dance hits you, and you have no choice but to respond by dancing. In fact, a song has been written about it; the song is appropriately named "Boogie Fever". Here are the first four lines:

Boogie fever
Got to boogie down
Boogie fever
I think it's going around

While I believe it is good to sing and dance, it is possible to take any good thing too far, and some people have taken dancing so far that they danced until they literally dropped dead. Sometimes it is just one person who starts dancing uncontrollably- in modern society, we would call that person insane and treat the person accordingly - who is engaging in such suicidal behavior. However, groups have engaged in such a behavior as well. The largest instance of dance fever on record occurred in Strasbourg, part of the Holy Roman Empire at the time, in August 1518.

When people get a severe case of boogie fever like they got in Strasbourg, they can't wait for the club like most of us; they just start dancing where they are like they do in those musicals where people constantly break out into song and dance. The Strasbourg dance party began in July when Frau Troffea began to silently twirl, twist, and shake. She danced by herself for almost a week, but by the end of the week 36-or-so other residents had joined dancing with her. The doctors were called but they didn't know what to make of it. They figured that the dancers would eventually tire; therefore, they suggested adding a band and letting the dancers continue until they wore themselves out.

It sounded like a good idea, but no matter what the doctors and government authorities did, the dancers did not get their fill of dancing. The dancers did not quit because of muscle fatigue; they quit because of heart attacks, strokes, and exhaustion. Finally, in September, after nearly 400 deaths, the remaining dancers were led up to a mountain retreat to a shrine where they prayed for forgiveness and for release of whatever possessed them. The absolution worked, and these dancers walked home to resume their daily duties.

No one can deny the dancing or the deaths, but what caused the spontaneous dancing and the resulting deaths? The local residents who were superstitious believed it was the curse of a good spirit or perhaps the work of an evil spirit; they point out that absolution put an end to it. (I wonder if they called the evil spirit the Boogie Man.) Are there alternative causes besides spirits? Although the residents of Strasbourg might not have seen any, sitting here today with all of the advances in psychology, we can argue that there are. One, the dance mania could have been psychological. The citizens of the village believed St. Vitus, a Roman Catholic saint, had the power to curse people with a dancing plague, and, because the residents could see that disease and famine were already all around them, it would make sense for the dancing plague to come too. The residents could have fallen into a group-think psychological mentality, believing that those around them believed in the curse and therefore they too should behave as if they were cursed or risk the wrath of the others; when presented with the option to no longer have to pretend to be something they were not, they quit pretending to be under the curse. A second explanation is that they accidently ingested something that produced spasms and/or hallucinations. The third explanation is that they deliberately ingested something to produce spasms and/or hallucinations (as many people do with recreational drugs today).

Cases of dance fever have also been found in Switzerland, Holland, and Germany, but none have involved as many people or been as deadly as the outbreak in Strasbourg. Like the dance fever in Strasbourg, no specific cause-and-effect source for these outbreaks has been determined. In all cases, witnesses say that the people's feet just got the urge to flop, and the owner had no choice but to obey. (People's feet may not flop uncontrollably today, but I have met many people whose mouths seem to have an uncontrollable desire to flop. My sixth grader teacher thought I talked too much; I should have told her that I was under the control of a spirit just like the people of Strasbourg were.) Do you sense the spirit of boogie coming on? Let's boogie on to the next article.

CHAPTER 31

WOULD YOU BELIEVE...

A LIVING MAN WENT FIVE WEEKS WITHOUT A PULSE – OR A HEART?

"Every day holds the possibility of a miracle."
- Elizabeth David

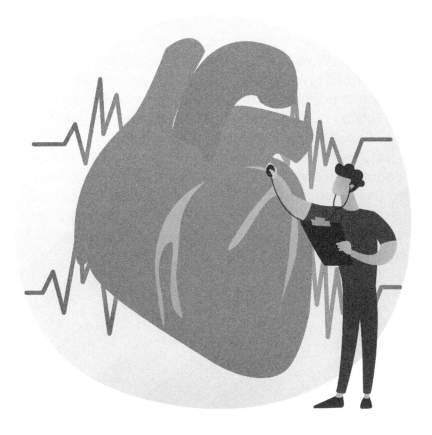

Let's do a quick quiz. If a young man is with a young woman and she faints, what should he instinctively touch on her? I'll give you three out of the five letters of the answer: P-U-_-S-_. Can you solve the puzzle?

If you answered "P-U-L-S-E" you are correct. If you said anything else, you are either very perverted or a very bad speller - perhaps both. I had a friend that said that as long as a woman had a pulse, he would go out with her no matter how she looked. He said that in front of one of my other friends who worked at the morgue and replied that a woman didn't even have to have a pulse to interest him. (I hope he was talking about one of those people who are running around without a heart and not referring to being a necrophiliac - I didn't dare ask. You do realize that science has come so far that people do not need beating hearts, don't you? Since they are fully functional human beings but have no heart, they literally have no pulse.)

I had heard of heartless people before I explored this topic in detail. Heartless people are the landlords who throw out their tenants in a snowstorm, the employers who conduct a mass firing right before Christmas, and the bullies who take candy from babies. Technically, these are not heartless people, they do have a heart – they just lack empathy. However, real heartless people are likely to live in the future; one man has already - Craig Lewis.

Craig had just turned 54 in 2012, a relatively youthful age for most people in that time period, but his heart was on the verge of expiring because of a build-up of abnormal proteins. All the doctors at the Texas Heart Institute concluded that a pacemaker could not save him, and most doctors had written him off as dead. However, a couple of doctors offered hope. Dr. Billy Cohn and Dr. Bud Frazier talked with Craig's wife. Craig was in a coma, she agreed to an experimental treatment on Craig's behalf. Billy and Bud had invented a device that allowed for a continuous flow of blood rather than the pumping of blood. The treatment had worked in over 50 calves but had never been tested on a person. When other doctors pronounced that Craig was down to his final twelve hours of life without their intervention, the two surgeons set to work.

By intricately tying two ventricular assist devices to form one device, they were able to replace Craig's entire heart. He had no heart, and therefore he had no pulse. Curious as to what he had if he did not have a pulse, his wife listened for his pulse and, where there used to be a pulse, she now heard a hum.

The treatment worked! Craig was awake the next day and was able to talk to the doctors. Craig lived five more weeks, and his new circulatory system would have likely taken him far beyond that. However, during those five weeks, his kidneys and liver continued to erode from the initial disease, so the family made the painful choice of turning the device off so he could have a humane death.

Billy and Bud's device may be the way of the future. Currently, people who need a heart replacement have the choice of artificial hearts or transplants; Billy and Bud's device provides a third choice. The device is currently being used in combination with the other two methods, and more data is being obtained about it.

The most famous person with an artificial heart and a Billy and Bud device inside him is George W. Bush's Vice President, Dick Cheney. Artificial hearts are just machines; machines that have to beat 100,000 times per day - that's 36,500,000 per year. Artificial hearts wear down, just as cars and other machines do, and the Billy and Bud device placed alongside an artificial heart helps the artificial heart to last lots longer by helping to control clotting, bleeding, and thrombosis.

I constantly tell my girlfriend, "My heart beats for you." Should I one day not have a heart and still want to express my love by referring to my circulatory system, I will tell her sweet nothings such as "I go with the flow when I'm around you" and "I may not have a heart, but I circulate around you just fine." These don't quite have the same ring to them as "my heart beats for you", but I'm sure the fine folks at Hallmark will be able to salvage Valentine's Day. Our society will eventually be full of older, heartless people, but, ironically, the beat will go on.

CHAPTER 32

WOULD YOU BELIEVE . . .

THE FIRST HUMAN TO RETURN FROM SPACE WAS BELIEVED TO BE A SPACE ALIEN WHEN HE LANDED BACK ON EARTH??

"There may be aliens in our Milky Way galaxy, and there are billions of other galaxies. The probability is almost certain that there is life somewhere in space."
- Buzz Aldrin

Have you ever feared being mistaken for something you are not? I have that fear all the time. I am an American citizen, and I love the colors red, white, and blue - except when they belong to the police car that is following me. Every time a police officer tails me, I fear that they perceive that I am a lawbreaker, that they are secretly running my license plate as they follow me and trying to find an excuse to pull me over. I know I am not a crook, but I wonder if the officers tailing me know it.

One of the worst cases of mistaken identity took place on April 12, 1961. On that day the first human in space - or at least the first human to return coherent from space - a cosmonaut named Yuri Gagarin, was mistaken for an outer space alien when he returned to earth.

The rural Russian farmers who saw Yuri land believed he was a creature from outer space coming to possibly terrorize the earth. Having just had the time of his life in space, Yuri now had to fear for his life on earth in a case of mistaken identity. As he approached the farmers - still in his spacesuit and his parachute dragging behind him, Yuri could see the fear in their eyes. The farmers stepped backward as he stepped toward them, their senses trying to decide between flight-or-fight. Yuri tried to put them at ease, saying in Russian, "Don't be afraid. I am a Soviet like you. I have descended from space, and I must find a telephone to call Moscow!"

Yuri was an instant international celebrity. He received the U.S.S.R.'s highest honor, the Hero of the Soviet Union. His popularity became so great that the Soviet premier, Leonid Brezhnev, became jealous. The Soviet elites were also unhappy with his message - while in space looking at the world, he concluded the world was small and that war had no place; his message of peace, hope, and love put other nations at ease about the U.S.S.R.'s intention in space, but it didn't stress that Mother Russia was the best land in the world and that others should bow down to it. Yuri may have had a third strike against him as well - he had inside knowledge of the Soviet space program, and rumors had begun to leak that he was not the first person in space - he was the first person to go into space and come back in the same condition he left. (Supposedly three or so cosmonauts had died in space, and another had crashed into China upon re-entry, resulting in a coma that the Soviets said was from a car accident.)

Perhaps it was an accident - or perhaps it was a murder made to look like an accident, but Yuri died in 1968 when the MIG-15 training jet he was piloting crashed. A machine like no other ever built and his piloting skills had kept him alive in space, but his trust in machines and in his piloting skills- or perhaps in human nature - ultimately did him in.

DID YOU ENJOY THE BOOK?

If you did, we are ecstatic. If not, please write your complaint to us and we will ensure we fix it.

Please email us at
chilimac@chilimacbooks.com

If you're feeling generous, there is something important that you can help us with – tell other people that you enjoyed the book.

ABOUT CHILI MAC BOOKS

Chili Mac Books is a small but fire crackin' publisher bringing hot stories of old back to life. Honing in on fascinating people, places, and events in history is their expertise with a mission to provide the tales of the extraordinary into the hands of curious minds around the world.

Whether highlighting legends of war, mavericks from around the world, or wacky stories you almost won't believe are true, Chili Mac Books lives to seek them out for the enjoyment of their loyal readers.

REFERENCES

Anderson, J., & Van Atta, D. (1989, September 20). Nuclear bombs to divert Soviet rivers? The Washington Post. Retrieved October 19, 2021, from https://www.washingtonpost.com/archive/lifestyle/1989/09/20/nuclear-bombs-to-divert-soviet-rivers/c9f97617-c653-4b75-b9f6-03c6bc80cf0e/.

Andrews, E. (2015, August 31). What was the dancing plague of 1518? History.com. Retrieved October 19, 2021, from https://www.history.com/news/what-was-the-dancing-plague-of-1518.

Andrews, E. (2016, October 31). What killed Harry Houdini? History.com. Retrieved October 19, 2021, from https://www.history.com/news/what-killed-harry-houdini.

Basilan, R. (2021, July 9). Michael Massee was the man who accidentally took Brandon Lee's life on set of 'the crow'. news.amomama.com. Retrieved October 19, 2021, from https://news.amomama.com/267714-michael-massee-the-man-who-accidentally.html.

Basilan, R. (2021, July 9). Michael Massee was the man who accidentally took Brandon Lee's life on set of 'the crow'. news.amomama.com. Retrieved October 19, 2021, from https://news.amomama.com/267714-michael-massee-the-man-who-accidentally.html.

BBC. (n.d.). A giant aircraft carrier built from Ice. BBC Future. Retrieved October 19, 2021, from https://www.bbc.com/future/article/20180323-a-giant-aircraft-carrier-built-of-ice.

Breaking Asia. (2020, July 3). Yoshie Shiratori: The incredible story of a man no prison could hold. Medium. Retrieved October 19, 2021, from https://medium.com/breakingasia/yoshie-shiratori-the-incredible-story-of-a-man-no-prison-could-hold-6d79a67345f5.

Buckingham Palace by A.A. Milne. by A.A. Milne - Famous poems, famous poets. - All Poetry. (n.d.). Retrieved October 19, 2021, from https://allpoetry.com/Buckingham-Palace.

Burris, C. (n.d.). Billy Possum. The Teacher's Toolbox: A Blog for Educators | Ohio History Connection. Retrieved October 19, 2021, from https://www.ohiohistory.org/learn/education/resource-roundup/november-2019-(1)/billy-possum.

Cardiga, M. (2021, June 23). Inside the double tragedy of Bruce Lee and his son Brandon both dying before 33. news.amomama.com. Retrieved October 19, 2021, from https://news.amomama.com/266304-bruce-brandon-lee-death-tragedy.html.

Carlos Jr., M. (n.d.). Yoshie Shiratori: The incredible story of a man no prison could hold. Breaking Asia. Retrieved October 19, 2021, from https://www.breakingasia.com/gov/yoshie-shiratori-the-incredible-story-of-a-man-no-prison-could-hold/.

Chris. (2017, March 10). Bubble wrap: A short history. The Packaging Company. Retrieved October 19, 2021, from https://www.thepackagingcompany.us/knowledge-sharing/bubble-wrap-short-history.

Crookes, D., & All About Space Magazine. (2021, April 12). Yuri Gagarin: How the first man in space sparked a conspiracy theory. Space.com. Retrieved October 19, 2021, from https://www.space.com/yuri-gagarin-conspiracy-theory.

Daily Mail Reporter. (2011, June 17). Craig Lewis's beatless heart: Texas husband lives 5 weeks without a pulse. Daily Mail Online. Retrieved October 19, 2021, from https://www.dailymail.co.uk/health/article-2003956/Craig-Lewiss-beatless-heart-Texas-husband-lives-5-weeks-pulse.html#.

Daily Mail Reporter. (2012, February 26). Meet the first heartless man who is able to live without a heartbeat or a pulse. Daily Mail Online. Retrieved October 19, 2021, from https://www.dailymail.co.uk/news/article-2096314/Meet-HEARTLESS-man-able-live-heartbeat-PULSE.html.

Demain, B. (2020, August 21). Smooth operator: How con man "count" Victor Lustig sold the Eiffel Tower-twice. Mental Floss. Retrieved October 19, 2021, from https://www.mentalfloss.com/article/12809/smooth-operator-how-victor-lustig-sold-eiffel-tower.

Do not pass go: The secret history of monopoly. Oxford Games. (2018, October 15). Retrieved October 19, 2021, from https://oxfordgames.co.uk/do-not-pass-go-the-secret-history-of-monopoly/.

Elliott, S. K. (n.d.). Antiques Roadshow. PBS. Retrieved October 19, 2021, from https://www.pbs.org/wgbh/roadshow/stories/articles/2015/3/20/how-teddy-bear-got-his-name.

Emile Leray survived the desert by building a motorcycle from his broken car. HistoryGarage. (2021, August 6). Retrieved October 19, 2021, from https://historygarage.com/emile-leray-survived-the-desert-by-building-a-motorcycle-from-his-broken-car/.

Encyclopædia Britannica, inc. (n.d.). Anne Bonny. Encyclopædia Britannica. Retrieved October 19, 2021, from https://www.britannica.com/biography/Anne-Bonny.

Foster, C. (2021, March 4). The fascinating, tragic dancing plague of 1518 that killed 400 people. Dusty Old Thing. Retrieved October 19, 2021, from https://dustyoldthing.com/dancing-plague-1518/#:⊠:text=Chris%20Foster-,In%20July%20of%201518%2C%20in%20the%20town%20of%20Strasbourg%2C%20Alsace,continued%20for%20six%20days%20straight.

Friel, M. (2020, November 25). What 'the Crown' got wrong about the intruder who broke into the Queen's bedroom in Buckingham Palace. Insider. Retrieved October 19, 2021, from https://www.insider.com/the-crown-michael-fagan-broke-into-queens-room-buckingham-palace-2020-11.

Garraffo, N. (2016, September 27). The history of Bubble wrap. A.B. Richards. Retrieved October 19, 2021, from https://www.abrichards.com/blog/the-history-of-bubble-wrap.

Graff, V. (2016, October 14). What's your perfect quirky sport? The Telegraph. Retrieved October 19, 2021, from https://www.telegraph.co.uk/only-in-britain/perfect-quirky-sports/.

Great Seal Bug. The thing. (n.d.). Retrieved October 19, 2021, from https://www.cryptomuseum.com/covert/bugs/thing/index.htm.

Grundhauser, E. (2017, November 14). The sad tale of the 'flying tailor.' Atlas Obscura. Retrieved October 19, 2021, from https://www.atlasobscura.com/articles/flying-tailor-eiffel-paris-france-parachute.

Guardian News and Media. (2015, April 11). The secret history of monopoly: The capitalist board game's leftwing origins. The Guardian. Retrieved October 19, 2021, from https://www.theguardian.com/lifeandstyle/2015/apr/11/secret-history-monopoly-capitalist-game-leftwing-origins.

Harford, T. (2019, August 20). The Cold War spy technology which we all use. BBC News. Retrieved October 19, 2021, from https://www.bbc.com/news/business-48859331.

Head, S. (2016, April 27). Seeing double: The fake paris of the First World War. Culture Trip. Retrieved October 19, 2021, from https://theculturetrip.com/europe/france/paris/articles/seeing-double-the-fake-paris-of-the-first-world-war/.

Hiskey, D. (2012, November 16). Happy bubble wrap appreciation day! Mental Floss. Retrieved October 19, 2021, from https://www.mentalfloss.com/article/13092/bubble-wrap-was-originally-supposed-be-wallpaper.

History of toe wrestling: Toe Wrestling History Information: Toe wrestling game history. Sports Know How. (2021, August 2). Retrieved October 19, 2021, from https://sportsmatik.com/sports-corner/sports-know-how/toe-wrestling/history.

History.com Editors. (2010, February 9). Soviet cosmonaut Yuri Gagarin becomes the first man in space. History.com. Retrieved October 19, 2021, from https://www.history.com/this-day-in-history/first-man-in-space.

Hollingsworth, J. (2020, August 9). This New Zealand city has an official wizard. he even gets paid. CNN. Retrieved October 19, 2021, from https://www.cnn.com/2020/08/08/asia/new-zealand-wizard-intl-hnk-dst/index.html.

IMDb.com. (n.d.). The crow. IMDb. Retrieved October 19, 2021, from https://www.imdb.com/title/tt0109506/plotsummary. Interesting Facts. (n.d.). 10 people who live without heart - youtube. Retrieved October 19, 2021, from https://www.youtube.com/watch?v=ZPxZarjhHKc.

Jenni, J. (2021, October 12). 13 facts about the monopoly man (aka mr. monopoly & rich uncle pennybags). Monopoly Land. Retrieved October 19, 2021, from https://www.monopolyland.com/monopoly-man-13-facts-about-mr-monopoly-aka-rich-uncle-pennybags/.

Johnson, B. (n.d.). The London Beer Flood of 1814. Historic UK. Retrieved October 19, 2021, from https://www.historic-uk.com/HistoryUK/HistoryofBritain/The-London-Beer-Flood-of-1814/.

Knapp, F. (2019, May 14). The curious career of living as a real-life garden gnome. Messy Nessy Chic. Retrieved October 19, 2021, from https://www.messynessychic.com/2019/05/14/the-curious-career-of-living-as-a-real-life-garden-gnome/.

Layton, J. (2008, April 30). How could someone steal a painting from a museum? HowStuffWorks. Retrieved October 19, 2021, from https://people.howstuffworks.com/steal-painting-from-museum.html.

Leff, G. (2021, January 26). This flight attendant fell from 33,000 feet - and lived for 44 years. View from the Wing. Retrieved October 19, 2021, from https://viewfromthewing.com/flight-attendant-fell-33000-feet-lived-44-years/.

Magazine, S. (2013, April 25). Russia's Cold War plan to reverse the ocean and melt the Arctic. Smithsonian.com. Retrieved October 19, 2021, from https://www.smithsonianmag.com/smart-news/russias-cold-war-plan-to-reverse-the-ocean-and-melt-the-arctic-42136682/.

Magazine, S. (2015, January 1). Monopoly was designed to teach the 99% about income inequality. Smithsonian.com. Retrieved October 19, 2021, from https://www.smithsonianmag.com/arts-culture/monopoly-was-designed-teach-99-about-income-inequality-180953630/.

Maryam. (2021, March 13). Knocker-uppers history: The Alarm Clock of the old century. Medium. Retrieved October 19, 2021, from https://historyofyesterday.com/knocker-uppers-history-the-alarm-clock-of-the-old-century-7224a610a538.

McArdle, T. (2019, October 21). How the 1911 theft of the mona lisa made it the world's most famous painting. The Washington Post. Retrieved October 19, 2021, from https://www.washingtonpost.com/history/2019/10/20/how-theft-mona-lisa-made-it-worlds-most-famous-painting/.

McNamee, G. (2021, April 12). The Soviet cosmonaut who was the first human in space. CNN. Retrieved October 19, 2021, from https://www.cnn.com/2021/04/12/world/space-race-yuri-gagarin-scn/index.html.

Mediratta, S. (1970, January 1). Bubble wrap was originally designed to be used as wallpaper. Inshorts. Retrieved October 19, 2021, from https://inshorts.com/en/news/bubble-wrap-was-originally-designed-to-be-used-as-wallpaper-1485850766792#⌷:text=Bubble%20wrap%20was%20originally%20designed%20to%20be%20used%20as%20wallpaper&text=Bubble%20wrap%20was%20invented%20in,that%20air%20bubbles%20were%20captured.

Neuharth, S. (2021, January 12). Fact checker: Did explorer Peter Freuchen save his life with a poop chisel? MeatEater Conservation. Retrieved October 19, 2021, from https://www.themeateater.com/conservation/anthropology/fact-checker-did-explorer-peter-freuchen-save-his-life-with-a-poop-chisel.

Nolasco, S. (2019, January 5). Harry Houdini's great-nephew explains why he wanted to explore late magician's secrets in docuseries. Fox News. Retrieved October 19, 2021, from https://www.foxnews.com/entertainment/harry-houdinis-great-nephew-explains-why-he-wanted-to-explore-magicians-secrets-in-docuseries.

Norman, A. (2017, August 16). Garden Gnomes were once real people employed as decoration by the rich. Business Insider. Retrieved October 19, 2021, from https://www.businessinsider.com/garden-gnomes-were-once-real-people-employed-as-decoration-by-the-rich-2017-8.

Oberg, J. (2008, February 12). Russia has the corner on guns in space. NBCNews.com. Retrieved October 19, 2021, from https://www.nbcnews.com/id/wbna23131359.

Ouellette, J. (2019, September 16). Knives made of frozen feces don't make the cut, disproving well-known legend. Ars Technica. Retrieved October 19, 2021, from https://arstechnica.com/science/2019/09/knives-made-of-frozen-feces-dont-make-the-cut-disproving-well-known-legend/.

Patowary, K. (2020, December 15). Franz Reichelt's fatal jump. Amusing Planet. Retrieved October 19, 2021, from https://www.amusingplanet.com/2020/12/franz-reichelts-fatal-jump.html.

Peek, S. (2016, March 27). Knocker uppers: Waking up the workers in Industrial Britain. BBC News. Retrieved October 19, 2021, from https://www.bbc.com/news/uk-england-35840393.

Pozniak, H. (2016, July 7). It's been voted Europe's most unmissable festival. The Telegraph. Retrieved October 19, 2021, from https://www.telegraph.co.uk/only-in-britain/worm-charming-guide/.

Preskar, P. (2021, March 25). The Knocker-upper-the extinct profession of waking people up by knocking. Medium. Retrieved October 19, 2021, from https://medium.com/lessons-from-history/knocker-upper-47bc8c5bfdbf.

Prisco, J. (2018, April 26). Project Habbakuk: Britain's secret attempt to build an ice warship. CNN. Retrieved October 19, 2021, from https://www.cnn.com/style/article/project-habbakuk-ice-aircraft-carrier/index.html.

Reilly, L. (2013, June 10). Billy Possum: President Taft's answer to the teddy bear. Mental Floss. Retrieved October 19, 2021, from https://www.mentalfloss.com/article/51030/billy-possum-president-tafts-answer-teddy-bear.

Rosenwald, M. (2020, November 17). Fact-checking 'the Crown': What the man who broke into the Queen's bedroom really wanted. The Washington Post. Retrieved October 19, 2021, from https://www.washingtonpost.com/history/2020/11/17/the-crown-michael-fagan-queen-elizabeth/#⌷:text=Inside%20England%2C%20the%20word%20conjures,on%20thrones%20and%20admiring%20paintings.

Sandomir, R. (2016, December 29). Vesna Vulovic, flight attendant who survived jetliner blast, dies at 66. The New York Times. Retrieved October 19, 2021, from https://www.nytimes.com/2016/12/28/world/europe/vesna-vulovic-died-flight-attendant-in-plunge.html.

Simple History. (n.d.). How did this convict escape prison using miso ... - youtube. Retrieved October 19, 2021, from https://www.youtube.com/watch?v=HG2GPqPJ13A.

Simple History. (n.d.). Human garden gnome (weird jobs in history) - youtube. Human Garden Gnome (Weird Jobs in History). Retrieved October 19, 2021, from https://www.youtube.com/watch?v=nOkACr7Zybk.

Simple History. (n.d.). Ice ship (secret weapon of WWII) - youtube. Retrieved October 19, 2021, from https://www.youtube.com/watch?v=xKZr2jMSagU.

Simple History. (n.d.). Knocker-upper (weird jobs in history) - youtube. Retrieved October 19, 2021, from https://www.youtube.com/watch?v=uOWhdm7Glrc.

Simple History. (n.d.). Leech collector (worst jobs in history) - youtube. Retrieved October 19, 2021, from https://www.youtube.com/watch?v=erCp⊠aHg9Sk.

Simple History. (n.d.). Strange deaths in history (20th century) - youtube. Retrieved October 19, 2021, from https://www.youtube.com/watch?v=44V6RFHnM1E.

Simple History. (n.d.). Strange famous deaths in history - youtube. Retrieved October 19, 2021, from https://www.youtube.com/watch?v=XHJfKAKIEig.

Simple History. (n.d.). The electrician who escaped the desert by ... - youtube.com. The Electrician who escaped the desert by turning his car into a motorbike. Retrieved October 19, 2021, from https://www.youtube.com/watch?v=BrRuWXSEP9E.

Simple History. (n.d.). The explorer who used a knife made of his own ... - youtube. The Explorer who used a Knife made of his own Poop to Escape from the Ice. Retrieved October 19, 2021, from https://www.youtube.com/watch?v=pIIO-GOjc20.

Simple History. (n.d.). The London Beer Flood of 1814 (strange stories) - youtube. Retrieved October 19, 2021, from https://www.youtube.com/watch?v=96OMuA65goo.

Simple History. (n.d.). The Soldier Bear (Strange Stories of World War II) - youtube. Retrieved October 19, 2021, from https://www.youtube.com/watch?v=0lu4rW0xaZQ.

Simple History. (n.d.). The stewardess who fell 33,000 feet and survived! (Flight 367) - youtube. Retrieved October 19, 2021, from https://www.youtube.com/watch?v=xhMkWGi0qKw.

Simple History. (n.d.). The stolen tank rampage! (1995) - youtube. Retrieved October 19, 2021, from https://www.youtube.com/watch?v=1aA90M0APBY.

Simple History. (n.d.). Tosher / Sewer Hunter (worst jobs in history) - youtube. Retrieved October 19, 2021, from https://www.youtube.com/watch?v=IMNRQix⊠QzQ.

Simple History. (n.d.). What was 'The thing'? (weird tech) - youtube. Retrieved October 19, 2021, from https://www.youtube.com/watch?v=sjnvHqoVxGQ.

Simple History. (n.d.). Yuri Gagarin, first human in space (1961) - youtube. Retrieved October 19, 2021, from https://www.youtube.com/watch?v=7iMa03BApcQ.

Skelley, J. (2020, August 31). So, New Zealand has a government-appointed wizard. BuzzFeed. Retrieved October 19, 2021, from https://www.buzzfeed.com/jemimaskelley/the-wizard#⊠:text=29%20Apr%202015-,So%2C%20New%20Zealand%20Has%20A%20Government%2DAppointed%20Wizard,legal%20name%20is%20The%20Wizard.

Smithsonian Magazine. (2012, June 29). Quite likely the worst job ever. Smithsonian.com. Retrieved October 19, 2021, from https://www.smithsonianmag.com/history/quite-likely-the-worst-job-ever-319843/.

Smithsonian Magazine. (2016, March 9). The man who sold the Eiffel Tower. twice. Smithsonian.com. Retrieved October 19, 2021, from https://www.smithsonianmag.com/history/man-who-sold-eiffel-tower-twice-180958370/.

Smithsonian Magazine. (2017, August 4). This 1814 beer flood killed eight people. Smithsonian.com. Retrieved October 19, 2021, from https://www.smithsonianmag.com/smart-news/1814-beer-flood-killed-eight-people-180964256/.

Stilwell, B. (2021, July 26). This is why Soviet cosmonauts carried a shotgun into space. We Are The Mighty. Retrieved October 19, 2021, from https://www.wearethemighty.com/mighty-tactical/why-soviet-cosmonauts-carried-shotgun/.

Stilwell, B. (2021, March 19). A veteran stole a Patton tank and went on a rampage in 1995. We Are The Mighty. Retrieved October 19, 2021, from https://www.wearethemighty.com/mighty-history/veteran-tank-rampage-patton-tank/.

The Story Behind. (n.d.). The heart-melting story of Wojtek, the soldier bear - youtube. Retrieved October 19, 2021, from https://www.youtube.com/watch?v=twr38iHXYVw.

thepaak786. (n.d.). Boogie fever (midnight special 1976) - youtube. Retrieved October 19, 2021, from https://www.youtube.com/watch?v=YHKCHvpYq⬛8.

Thoughty2. (n.d.). How did one man steal the Mona Lisa in broad ... - youtube. Retrieved October 19, 2021, from https://www.youtube.com/watch?v=QWi1c-HWuIE.

Thoughty2. (n.d.). How One man sold the Eiffel Tower, twice... - youtube. Retrieved October 19, 2021, from https://www.youtube.com/watch?v=060WE73L3ao.

Thoughty2. (n.d.). How this man broke into Buckingham Palace twice ... - youtube. Retrieved October 19, 2021, from https://www.youtube.com/watch?v=1ljCpjIAW4w.

Thoughty2. (n.d.). They never stood a chance against this infamous pirate... - youtube. Retrieved October 19, 2021, from https://www.youtube.com/watch?v=34TbYS93oIU.

Thoughty2. (n.d.). Welcome to the weird world of competitive ... - youtube.com. Retrieved October 19, 2021, from https://www.youtube.com/watch?v=U78H8bWYFYw.

Thoughty2. (n.d.). Which country has a national wizard? rif 67 - youtube. Retrieved October 19, 2021, from https://www.youtube.com/watch?v=R3QiPQBQcSA.

Thoughty2. (n.d.). Why did everyone in 1518 dance themselves to ... - youtube. Retrieved October 19, 2021, from https://www.youtube.com/watch?v=Z9lqusiaQSo.

Thoughty2. (n.d.). Why was bubblewrap invented? rif 32 - youtube. Retrieved October 19, 2021, from https://www.youtube.com/watch?v=W0eHj9y⬛YRw.

Tilford, J. (2017, November 26). Leech collectors and the leech craze of the 1800s. Ripley's Believe It or Not! Retrieved October 19, 2021, from https://www.ripleys.com/weird-news/leech-collectors/.

Top 16 quotes by Yuri Gagarin: A-Z quotes. Yuri Gagarin Quotes. (n.d.). Retrieved October 19, 2021, from https://www.azquotes.com/author/5270-Yuri⬛Gagarin.

Van Huygen, M. (2019, June 18). The time the Soviets gave the U.S. a hidden spy device-and it took seven years to discover it. Mental Floss. Retrieved October 19, 2021, from https://www.mentalfloss.com/article/584493/soviet-spies-bugged-united-states-seven-years.

Vermillion, S. (2017, July 13). Inside England's annual Toe Wrestling Championship. Mental Floss. Retrieved October 19, 2021, from https://www.mentalfloss.com/article/502081/inside-englands-annual-toe-wrestling-championship.

Walton, G. (2019, May 18). London sewer hunters in the 1800s. Geri Walton. Retrieved October 19, 2021, from https://www.geriwalton.com/london-sewer-hunters/.

Walton, G. (2020, November 1). Leech collectors or leech gatherers: An unusual occupation. Geri Walton. Retrieved October 19, 2021, from https://www.geriwalton.com/the-unusual-occupation-of-the-leech-collectors-or-leech-gatherers/.

Waxman, O. B. (2017, April 8). Wojtek the bear: Surprising World War II animal hero. Time. Retrieved October 19, 2021, from https://time.com/4731787/wojtek-the-bear-history/.

Welkos, R. W. (1993, April 1). Bruce Lee's son, Brandon, killed in movie accident. Los Angeles Times. Retrieved October 19, 2021, from https://www.latimes.com/archives/la-xpm-1993-04-01-mn-17681-story.html#:⬛:text=Actor%20Brandon%20Lee%2C%20the%2028,movie%20set%20in%20Wilmington%2C%20N.C.

Well-behaved women seldom make history Anne Bonny profile. (n.d.). Retrieved October 19, 2021, from https://www.pbs.org/newshour/extra/app/uploads/2014/02/Anne-Bonny-Profile-w-A.pdf.

We're off to see the wizard. Judy Garland - We're Off To See The Wizard Lyrics | Lyrics.com. (n.d.). Retrieved October 19, 2021, from https://www.lyrics.com/lyric/751764/Judy+Garland/We're+off+to+See+the+Wizard.

Why did cosmonauts take shotguns into space? - youtube. Simple History. (n.d.). Retrieved October 19, 2021, from https://www.youtube.com/watch?v=qRC0Jmh-9tY.

Wikimedia Foundation. (2021, August 12). Bubble wrap (brand). Wikipedia. Retrieved October 19, 2021, from https://www.en.wikipedia.org/wiki/Bubble_Wrap_(brand).

Wikimedia Foundation. (2021, June 29). Parachute pants. Wikipedia. Retrieved October 19, 2021, from https://en.wikipedia.org/wiki/Parachute_pants#.

Wikimedia Foundation. (2021, October 12). Vincenzo Peruggia. Wikipedia. Retrieved October 19, 2021, from https://en.wikipedia.org/wiki/Vincenzo_Peruggia.

Wikimedia Foundation. (2021, October 16). Brandon Lee. Wikipedia. Retrieved October 19, 2021, from https://en.wikipedia.org/wiki/Brandon_Lee.

Wikimedia Foundation. (2021, October 17). Michael Fagan (intruder). Wikipedia. Retrieved October 19, 2021, from https://en.wikipedia.org/wiki/Michael_Fagan_(intruder).

Wikimedia Foundation. (2021, October 17). Yuri Gagarin. Wikipedia. Retrieved October 19, 2021, from https://en.wikipedia.org/wiki/Yuri_Gagarin.

Wikimedia Foundation. (2021, October 4). Death of yuri gagarin. Wikipedia. Retrieved October 19, 2021, from https://en.wikipedia.org/wiki/Death_of_Yuri_Gagarin.

Wikimedia Foundation. (2021, October 4). Wojtek (bear). Wikipedia. Retrieved October 19, 2021, from https://en.wikipedia.org/wiki/Wojtek_(bear).

Wikimedia Foundation. (2021, October 5). Shawn Nelson (criminal). Wikipedia. Retrieved October 19, 2021, from https://en.wikipedia.org/wiki/Shawn_Nelson_(criminal).

Wikimedia Foundation. (2021, October 5). Vesna Vulović. Wikipedia. Retrieved October 19, 2021, from https://en.wikipedia.org/wiki/Vesna_Vulovi%C4%87.

Wikimedia Foundation. (2021, October 6). Bruce Lee. Wikipedia. Retrieved October 19, 2021, from https://en.wikipedia.org/wiki/Bruce_Lee.

Woody, C. (2018, September 26). The story of Wojtek, the 440-pound bear that fought the Nazis in World War II, is being made into a movie. Business Insider. Retrieved October 19, 2021, from https://www.businessinsider.com/story-of-wwii-polish-army-bear-wojtek-being-turned-into-film-2018-9.

Wynne, K. (2018, November 1). How did Harry Houdini die on Halloween? looking at his legacy 92 years after his death. Newsweek. Retrieved October 19, 2021, from https://www.newsweek.com/how-did-harry-houdini-die-halloween-looking-his-legacy-92-years-after-his-1195588.

Printed in Great Britain
by Amazon